Observations on Some Parts of the Answer of Earl Cornwallis to Sir Henry Clinton's Narrative

You are holding a reproduction of an original work that is in the public domain in the United States of America, and possibly other countries. You may freely copy and distribute this work as no entity (individual or corporate) has a copyright on the body of the work. This book may contain prior copyright references, and library stamps (as most of these works were scanned from library copies). These have been scanned and retained as part of the historical artifact.

This book may have occasional imperfections such as missing or blurred pages, poor pictures, errant marks, etc. that were either part of the original artifact, or were introduced by the scanning process. We believe this work is culturally important, and despite the imperfections, have elected to bring it back into print as part of our continuing commitment to the preservation of printed works worldwide. We appreciate your understanding of the imperfections in the preservation process, and hope you enjoy this valuable book.

OBSERVATIONS

ON

Some Parts of Earl Cornwallis's Answer

TO

Sir Henry Clinton's Narrative.

BY

LIEUTENANT-GENERAL
SIR HENRY CLINTON, K. B.

WHEN I published a Narrative of my conduct during the period of my command in North America, which comprehends the campaign of 1781, I was in hopes I had said every thing that was requisite to explain the motives of my own actions, and to convince every unprejudiced person, that certain positions respecting them, advanced in Lord Cornwallis's letter to me of the 20th of October, had no foundation. But it gives me extreme concern to observe, that his Lordship's seeming to avow nearly the same sentiments in his Introduction to a late publication, styled, an Answer to that Narrative, lays me under the necessity of troubling the public again upon a subject, which they are probably tired of; and I sincerely wished to have done with. I hope, therefore, it may not be judged improper to request their attention to the following Observations on some of the opinions and assertions therein stated. Which (to be as concise as possible) I shall take according to the order in which they occur;— adding only, in an Appendix, the copies of such extracts from my correspondence, and other papers, as appear necessary.

I find upon enquiry that the four letters were omitted to be sent to the Secretary of State, which Lord Cornwallis mentions to have been wanting when the papers relating to this business were laid before the House of Lords. But the reasons for his Lordship's

march

march from Cross-creek to Wilmington, and from thence into Virginia (stated in the first of them) had been before given in his letters of the 23d and 24th of April, to the Secretary of State, General Phillips, and myself; and these stand the first of those letters from his Lordship's correspondence, read before the House of Lords; the other three letters had been inserted in a pamphlet containing extracts from our correspondence, handed about at the time of the enquiry; and one of those pamphlets had been presented, by my order, to Lord Townshend, as a man of honour, and a friend to both parties, previous (I believe) to his noticing this omission to the House; and all the four missing letters were soon after published in the Parliamentary Register, along with those which had been read to the Lords. So that Lord Cornwallis could not well have sustained any injury by that omission. This, however, cannot be said to have been the case with mine of the 30th of November, and 2d of December to his Lordship, and of the 6th of December to the American Minister; which were with-held, whilst Lord Cornwallis's letters of the 20th of October, and 2d of December (to which they were anfwers) were fuffered to operate, for a long time, upon the minds of the public, to my prejudice.

My letters of the 30th of November and 2d of December, were in Lord Cornwallis's poffeffion, when his friend, Lord Townfhend, moved for thofe of his Lordfhip, which he judged neceffary to explain his conduct. The public will judge, whether mine were not, at leaft, equally fo, to explain mine; and whether, on finding that the Secretary of State had omitted to produce them to the Lords, Lord Cornwallis ought not to have defired Lord Townfhend to have moved for them. I declare, I would have done fo, had I been in his Lordfhip's place.

The four other letters, taken notice of by Lord Cornwallis, were certainly not delivered to him before November; becaufe the three firft, having been committed to the charge of General Leflie, (who was in a manner embarked for the Chefapeak, from the beginning of Auguft to the arrival of the French fleet) could not have been tranfmitted to his Lordfhip fooner; and the laft (the fubftance of which, however, had been previoufly communicated

in

in the prefence of a council of war, for his Lordfhip's information to Major Cockran, who joined him on the 9th of October) being fent by an advice boat, did not reach the Chefapeak before his furrender. But whoever will take the trouble of perufing thofe letters, will perceive that his Lordfhip's conduct (in the then ftate of matters) could not have been influenced by an earlier receipt of them.

Every man of fenfibility muft lament that Lord Cornwallis has fo indifcreetly availed himfelf of the liberty, he fuppofed was given him, by the late change in American meafures. For as *my fecret and moft private letter* to General Phillips, dated April 30, contained nothing neceffary for his Lordfhip's juftification; the publifhing it was highly impolitic at leaft, not to fay more — for reafons too obvious to need explanation.

No perfon can be more ready than I am to admit the difficulties Lord Cornwallis had to ftruggle with; and I fhall always acknowledge that I expected fuccefs (notwithftanding) from his Lordfhip's abilities. I left his Lordfhip in the Carolinas, with every power, civil and military, which I could give him, to carry on such

such operations as he should judge most likely to complete their reduction. Where I had hopes of success, I studiously sought to approve without reserve. And, as long as I imagined his Lordship to be in sufficient force, and in other respects prepared and competent to give the experiment of supporting our friends in North Carolina, *a fair and solid trial*, I certainly approved. But after the unfortunate day of *Cowpens*, which diminished his Lordship's acting army nearly one fourth; and after he thought proper to destroy great part of his waggons, proviant train, &c. (whereby he was reduced, I fear, to something too like a Tartar move); had it then been possible for him to have consulted me, he would have found that, could I have even *consented* to his persisting in his march into that province, that consent must have totally rested upon the high opinion I entertained of his Lordship's exertions, and not on any other flattering prospect I had of success.

Major Ferguson's misfortune was one of those untoward circumstances, which Lord Cornwallis says, occured during the four months succeeding the battle of Camden. His Lordship,

Lordship, immediately after the complete victory he there obtained, ordered our friends in North Carolina, to arm and intercept the beaten army of General Gates; promising them at the same time, that he would march directly to the borders of that province in their support. About this time Major Ferguson was detached to a distance from his Lordship, with a body of militia (without being supported by regular troops) under an idea that he could make them fight; notwithstanding his Lordship had informed me, some little time before, that it was contrary to the experience of the army, as well as of Major Ferguson himself. The consequence was, that the Major and his whole corps were unfortunately massacred. Lord Cornwallis was, immediately upon hearing of this event, obliged to quit the borders of North Carolina, and leave our friends there at the mercy of an inveterate enemy, whose power became irresistible by this necessary retreat. This fatal catastrophe, moreover, lost his Lordship the whole militia of Ninety-six, amounting to four thousand men, and even threw South Carolina into a state of confusion and rebellion.

wallis

OBSERVATIONS.

How nearly the force I left with Lord Cornwallis in the Southern district, and what I afterwards sent to him, might have been adequate or not to the success expected from it, I shall not now examine. It was all I could possibly spare. But for the satisfaction of the public, I shall give at the end of the Appendix, a view of the force first left with his Lordship, of what was sent to him afterwards, and of what was finally under his Lordship's orders throughout the whole extent of his command; — to contrast with which, I shall add also another view of the force left under my own immediate orders at New York, at different periods; giving at the same time as near a calculation as I can make from the intelligence received, of the number of regular troops which the enemy had opposed to each of us. I beg leave likewise to mention, that before I sailed from Charles-town, I offered to Lord Cornwallis all he wished, all he wanted, of every sort; and that his Lordship expressed himself to be perfectly satisfied with the troops he had, and wished for no more, as will appear from the letters annexed. What the exact strength of the corps under his Lordship's immediate command may have been at any given period,

period, I cannot afcertain, as I had not regular returns of them; but his Lordſhip did not make any complaint to me of the ſmallneſs of his force when he commenced his move into North Carolina; and I always thought it to be full as large as I had rated it at.

I cannot judge of the aſſurances of co-operation which Lord Cornwallis may have received from our friends in North Carolina, but from his Lordſhip's report; and his Lordſhip beſt knows, whether *he received any after the effects of Major Ferguſon's misfortune were known.* But his Lordſhip cannot forget that our friends, who had riſen by his order, were left expoſed to ruin by his retreat, and numbers of them actually maſſacred. I am therefore at a loſs to gueſs what may have been his Lordſhip's reaſons for being ſurprized that they failed to join him after the victory at Guildford; as ſuch effort of loyalty could ſcarcely be expected from them after their paſt ſufferings, when they ſaw his Lordſhip's army ſo greatly reduced after the action, and ſo ſcantily ſupplied with proviſions; which, without doubt was very far ſhort of that ſolid ſupport which they had been encouraged to expect from his

Lordſhip's

Lordship's promises. And indeed his Lordship might have supposed that these were their sentiments from what followed, as described by himself. "Many of the inhabitants rode "into camp, shook me by the hand, said "they were glad to see us, and to hear we had "beat Greene, and then rode home again;"— no doubt with aching hearts, from the melancholy scene his Lordship's camp "*encumbered* "*with a long train of sick and wounded,*" exhibited to their view.

But as this attempt (such as it was) had failed, surely Lord Cornwallis's next object should have been, *to secure South Carolina:* and this appears to have been his Lordship's own opinion when he wrote his letter to General Leslie of the 12th of December, 1780:— "We will then give our friends in North- "Carolina *a fair trial.* If they behave like "men, it may be of the greatest advantage to "the affairs of Britain. If they are as - - - - "as our friends to the southward, we must "leave them to their fate, and *secure what we* "*have got.*" Had I not consequently every reason to expect his Lordship would have done so? To what purpose then did his Lordship march

OBSERVATIONS.

march to Wilmington from Cross-creek, as he was so much nearer Camden and South Carolina? Or, even when at Wilmington, (as he could not but be apprehensive for the safety of South Carolina, from General Greene's march into that province; — and even for Charlestown,* *whose old works were in part levelled, to* " *make way for new ones, which were not yet* " *constructed; and whose garrison was inadequate* " *to oppose any force of consequence;*" which material information it is presumed Colonel Balfour could not have failed communicating to his Lordship as well as to Lord Rawdon,) why did not his Lordship retire to Charlestown by the route of Lockwood's folly and the Waggamaw? Which, it is the opinion of many others as well as mine, was practicable. For gallies might have secured him the passage of that river, and we then held the post of George-town upon its banks: it was, moreover, early in the month of April, long before the droughts set in, and it may therefore be presumed there was not much danger of the mills wanting water, as his Lordship seems to

have

* Vide Lord Rawdon's Letter to Lord Cornwallis, dated May 24, 1781.

have apprehended. Had his Lordship fortunately done so, South Carolina would have been saved, and the fatal catastrophe which afterwards happened to his army in the Chesapeak avoided. Lord Cornwallis in answer to this says, " that he decided to march into " Virginia, *as the safest and most effectual means* " *of employing the small corps under his command.* " For the force in South Carolina was in his " opinion sufficient, when collected, to secure " what was valuable to us in that province." But his Lordship's letter to General Phillips, of the 24th of April, (written a day or two before he moved) so far from representing this march *as a safe one*, describes it as most perilous. And if there was a possibility that his Lordship's return to South Carolina (even by sea) might prevent any material part of that province or Georgia from falling into the enemy's hands, (as many of the posts there did, notwithstanding his Lordship's opinion of the *sufficiency of the force to secure them,*) it may be presumed, that his Lordship's *march into Virginia was not the most effectual means of employing the corps under his command*, as the event has but too well proved to our cost. Lord Cornwallis

wallis gives likewife another reafon for this move. He fays, " he was influenced by ha-
" ving juft received an account from Charles-
" town of the arrival of a frigate with dif-
" patches from me. The fubftance of which
" then tranfmitted to him was, that General
" Phillips had been detached to the Chefa-
" peak, and put under his orders. Which in-
" duced him *to hope that folid operations might*
" *be adopted in that quarter.*" I fhall therefore take the liberty of faying a few words on this paffage, which appears to me very neceffary to be explained.

The difpatches his Lordfhip alludes to, were my letters to his Lordfhip of the 2d, 5th, and 8th, of March, with a copy of my inftructions to General Phillips. Captain Amherft, of the Sixtieth regiment, having charged him-felf with thofe of Lord Cornwallis, and other difpatches for Colonel Balfour, failed from New-York on the 20th of March, in a merchant fhip, called the Jupiter. And as Colonel Balfour acknowledged the receipt of them all, in his letter to me of the 7th of April, it is prefumable they were delivered to him on or before that day. This letter was brought to

me

me by his Majesty's ship Amphitrite; which, having in her way called at Cape Fear, brought me a letter likewise from Lord Cornwallis, at Wilmington, dated the 10th of April. It is therefore to be lamented, that neither the dispatches themselves, nor the substance of them, had been transmitted to his Lordship by that ship. The Speedy packet too, which was sent from Charles-town soon after the Amphitrite, with letters to me of the 20th of April, called likewise in her way at Cape Fear, and brought me letters from his Lordship of the 22d, 23d, and 24th of April; but I am concerned to observe, that safe opportunity of conveying my dispatches to his Lordship was also missed. Although Lord Cornwallis, in his letter to the American minister of the 23d April, and in his introduction, intimates that the substance of those dispatches was sent to him on the 22d April; I should, notwithstanding, suppose, that what was sent to his Lordship as such must have been improperly stated. For by having recourse to the dispatches at large, it will be seen, that so far from *inducing his Lordship to hope that solid operation might be adopted in Virginia,*

OBSERVATIONS.

(as he intimates the substance of them did) it is presumed, they would on the contrary have convinced him, that I had not even an idea of the sort (which, indeed, his Lordship might have already judged from my letter of 6th November) and therefore, instead of influencing his Lordship's move into that province, they might have most probably prevented it. But when the Public have read my letters to Lord Cornwallis of the 2d, 5th, and 8th of March, and my instructions to General Phillips, they will be competent to judge in what manner they were most likely to influence his Lordship; had he received them, or even the substance of them, before he commenced his march into Virginia, as I think his Lordship might have perceived by the *instructions* that Generals Phillips and Arnold, with part of the Chesapeak corps, were to be drawn back to New-York for a particular service, after a certain time;— and *by the letters*, that a considerable French armament was sailed from Rhode-island to the Chesapeak. It is consequently presumable, that in the *first instance* his Lordship would not have marched into Virginia, lest he should interfere

terfere with my plans; and that *in the other* he would have been equally cautious of doing so, *lest he should hazard the destruction of his own corps*, should the troops in Chesapeak happen at the time to be invested at Portsmouth, which from those letters would appear very probable to be the case.

I will frankly own that I ever disapproved of an attempt to conquer Virginia before the Carolinas were absolutely restored. However, when I saw that Lord Cornwallis had forced himself upon me in that province, I left him at liberty to act there as he judged best, as may appear by my letter to his Lordship of the 29th of May, which was the first I had an opportunity of writing to him after my knowledge of his arrival at Petersburg, or of his intentions of coming there.

Although Lord Cornwallis thought proper to decline engaging in the plan of operations which I had proposed to him in case he had none of his own; I am at a loss to guess what may be his motives for saying, " *I did not seem* " *inclined to take more share in the responsibility* " *than barely to recommend it*;" and indeed I cannot think his Lordship was really serious

in

OBSERVATIONS. 17

in fuggefting an infinuation fo apparently groundlefs. For it is manifeft that my letter to General Phillips of the 30th of April (publifhed by Lord Cornwallis) conveys to him and General Arnold the *moft explicit inftructions* for carrying thofe operations into execution; and it can fcarcely be doubted, that thofe inftructions were equally *explicit to his Lordfhip*, the moment the command of that army devolved upon him. Befides, though it may be admitted that I only *barely recommended* the move, in my letters on the fubject to his Lordfhip (becaufe it had been hitherto ufual for me to leave him to his own difcretion) yet I am perfuaded a reference to my correfpondence (as publifhed by Lord Cornwallis and myfelf) will fhew that thofe recommendations were fufficiently explicit to fix refponfibility upon me, had his Lordfhip adopted my plan, and afterwards failed.

Lord Cornwallis is pleafed to fay, " that
" he informed me he fhould repair to Wil-
" liamfburg, about the time when he fhould
" receive my anfwer, in order to be in readi-
" nefs to execute my commands; and that he
" fhould *employ the intermediate fpace* in de-
d " ftroying

"stroying such of the enemy's stores and ma-
"gazines as might be within his reach."—
The letter which is thus explained was dated
the 26th of May, at Byrd's, a little more than
twenty miles from Richmond, which is fifty
from Williamsburg, and is expressed in the
following words: " I shall *now* proceed to dis-
"lodge La Fayette *from Richmond*, and with
"my light troops to destroy any magazines
"or stores in the *neighbourhood*, which may
"have been collected either for his use or for
"General Greene's army. *From thence* I pur-
"pose to move to the *Neck at Williamsburg*,
"which is represented as healthy, and keep
"myself unengaged from operations which
"might interfere with your plan for the cam-
"paign, until I have the satisfaction of hear-
"ing from you. I hope I *shall then have an op-
"portunity to receive better information* than has
"hitherto been in my power to procure rela-
"tive to *a proper harbour and place of arms.*
"At present I am inclined to think well of
"York. *The objections to Portsmouth* are, *that
"it cannot be made strong without an army to de-
"fend it, that it is remarkably unhealthy, and can
"give no protection to a ship of the line.*" From
the

OBSERVATIONS.

the foregoing letter I naturally concluded, that, as soon as his Lordship had finished the service he was gone on, (which I did not imagine would have taken up above six or seven days at most) he would endeavour to *obtain information respecting a proper harbour and place of arms*; and having found it, that he was actually employed in establishing a post there. For, not having received any letter from his Lordship between the 26th of May and 30th of June, I was totally ignorant of his having changed his design, (as described in his letter of the first date) and *gone across the country towards Fredericksburg, by Hanover Court-house*; an operation which took his Lordship a complete month before he reached Williamsburg. But had his Lordship fortunately explained to me his instructions in that letter in the same manner he has now explained his letter, I should have seen that his Lordship had no idea of establishing a post on the Williamsburg Neck: and, when I found he had no plan of his own, would of course have sent early and explicit orders for that purpose, either to his Lordship, or in his absence to General Leslie, whereby much time might have been saved,

and

and the fatal cataſtrophe that followed—at leaſt retarded, by his Lordſhip being in a better ſtate of defence than that in which the enemy found him. For, though from his Lordſhip's letter to me of the 22d of Auguſt*, I had every reaſon to ſuppoſe that a proper ſurvey of the ground had been taken, and a judicious plan fixed on for fortifying it; I very much fear that nothing material was done until after the arrival of the French fleet on the 29th of Auguſt, as the engineer has ſince given me to underſtand (when I aſked him for his ſurvey) that he did not take one. There appears, therefore, to have been a miſapprehenſion ſomewhere reſpecting this matter, as well as the number of intrenching tools; which, though computed by his Lordſhip† to be

---

* *Extract.—Letter from Lord Cornwallis to Sir H. Clinton, dated York-Town, Auguſt 22, 1781.*

"The engineer has *finiſhed his ſurvey* and examination "of *this place*, and has propoſed his plan for fortifying it; "which, appearing judicious, I have approved of, and "directed to be executed."

† *Extract.—Letter from Lord Cornwallis to Sir H. Clinton dated York-Town, October 20, 1781.*

"And our ſtock of intrenching tools, which *did not* "*much exceed four hundred, when we began to work* in the "latter end of Auguſt, was now much diminiſhed."

be only about four hundred when he began to work on the York fide, I find by his engineer's reports, in my poffeffion, to have been 992* on the 23d of Auguft, the day on which (it is prefumed from the letter before quoted) he began to break ground.

Lord Cornwallis is alfo pleafed to fay, " Whoever reads the correfpondence will fee, " that fince Sir H. Clinton had declared pofi- " tively in his firft, and in feveral fubfequent " difpatches againft the plan for reducing " Virginia, no *explicit alternative* was left to " me, between complying with the requifition " (contained in his letters of the 11th and " 15th of June) of fuch troops as I could fpare " from a healthy defenfive ftation, or engaging " in operations in the Upper Chefapeak." But this conclufion does not, I prefume necefsarily follow; for though it is admitted that the whole of my correfpondence with the American Minifter and Lord Cornwallis uniformly declare my fentiments, of the impracticability of reducing Virginia by an operation folely there, without the good-will and aid of the inhabitants,—and of the bad policy

of

---

* Vide the return in the Appendix.

of the measure from the unhealthiness of the climate; and I was equally uniform in expressing to his Lordship my wishes, that he would adopt my ideas of the move to the Delaware Neck, &c. against which there were none of those objections. Yet, when I found that his Lordship was averse to engage in the operations concerted with General Phillips, and that he concurred with that officer respecting the propriety of changing the post of Portsmouth for one more healthy and defensible, I gave my consent to the change proposed, and referred his Lordship to my correspondence with General Phillips for my opinions thereon. His Lordship might have therefore judged that I expected he would immediately carry into execution this part of my plan, especially as his Lordship might have recollected that he told me in the letter before quoted, " That he hoped, when he got to the " Williamsburg Neck, he should have an op- " portunity to receive better information than " had hitherto been in his power to procure, " relative to a *proper harbour and place of* " *arms*." Wherefore, as his Lordship was left at liberty by my letters of the 11th and 15th

15th of June, to detain all the troops, if he had not finished the operations he was engaged in: and as his Lordship had *not completed his measures relative to a proper harbour and place of arms*, which appears from his letter to have been one of the operations he proposed engaging in; it may be fairly concluded that an *explicit alternative* was left him. For the letter of the 11th of June explicitly recommends to his Lordship *the taking a healthy defensive station* wherever he chose on the Williamsburg Neck; and only calls for what troops he could spare from its ample defence and other purposes mentioned, *after it was taken*. And as his Lordship *had not yet taken that station*, the troops were without doubt to be detained;— because *in that case only* my letter requested them to be sent; but though his Lordship might possibly have understood the letter differently at the time, we may at least suppose that, as it referred him to other letters of the 29th of May and 8th of June, for a further explanation of my wishes, and these letters had not then been received by his Lordship, he had very sufficient reason *to suspend at least* his intention of crossing James River, until he he either received them or heard again from New-York. Lord Cornwallis endeavours to invalidate this reasoning by saying, " that the " choice of a healthy station was controlled " by other material considerations, particularly " the *imminent danger of New-York*, and the im- " *portant effects expected from the expedition* " *against Philidelphia.*" His Lordship will, however, forgive me if I cannot discover from whence those considerations arose; as my letters of the 11th and 15th of June (which were the only letters *he had *then* received) do not describe New-York to *be in any sort of danger*, and his Lordship by his answer to those letters seemed of opinion, *that the project against Philadelphia was then become inexpedient*. I am therefore sorry to be under the necessity of repeating, that it is my opinion, his Lordship totally misconceived all my orders and intentions respecting this business, when he judged they warranted his *passing James River* and retiring to *Portsmouth*;—*which* I could not possibly suspect his Lordship would make choice of as a *healthy defensible station*,

after

---

* Vide his Lordship's letter of the 30th of June.

after he had juft told me in his letter of the 26th of May, " that it was *remarkably un-* " *healthy, and (though fortified) required an* " *army to defend it.*" But our correfpondence is now before the public, and they will judge whether my orders authorized his Lordfhip to do fo, and whether confequently fix weeks at leaft were not loft *in fecuring a place of arms*, which we both feemed to concur in opinion was neceffary. With refpect to his Lordfhip's faying, " It will be feen by the correfpondence " that the Commander-in-chief's opinion of " the indifpenfible neceffity of a harbour for " line of battle fhips only appears in his letter " of the 11th of July, after he had been ac- " quainted that the troops intended for the " expedition againft Philadelphia would be " foon ready to fail," (thereby intimating that it was a new idea juft then ftarted) I prefume it may be eafily made appear from the fame correfpondence, that fo far from being a new idea, *the taking a ftation for large fhips* was one of the earlieft and principal objects recommended to General Phillips's confideration and enquiry.* And I think it may be inferred,

from

---

* Vide inftructions of the 10th of March.

from his Lordship's objecting to Portsmouth, in the letter of the 26th of May, "*because it could not give protection to a ship of the line,*" that he regarded it as such, and consequently went in search of a naval station *as standing in that general officer's place*, it being apparently from that letter one of the principal reasons which induced his Lordship to go to the Williamsburg Neck.

Lord Cornwallis says, " Hampton-road was recommended by that order; but as it was upon examination found totally unfit for the purpose desired, every person can judge *whether the order did not then in its spirit become positive to occupy York and Gloucester.*" To enable every person therefore to judge whether it did or not, I shall beg leave to transcribe the words of the order. " I request that your Lordship will without loss of time *examine Old Point Comfort, and fortify it.* But if it should be your Lordship's opinion that Old Point Comfort *cannot be held without having possession of York,* for *in this case* Gloucester may perhaps be not so material) *and that the whole* cannot be done with less than seven thousand men, you are at full liberty to detain all the

" troops

"troops now in Chefapeak, which I believe
"amount to fomewhat more than that num-
"ber. Which very liberal conceffion will, I
"am perfuaded, convince your Lordfhip of
"the high eftimation in which I hold a naval
"ftation in Chefapeak." If nothing elfe had
been faid to Lord Cornwallis or General Phillips, upon the fubject of a naval ftation, but
what this order contains; there could not in
my humble opinion be a doubt, that his Lordfhip was not at liberty to take any other than
Old Point Comfort, — except he fhould be of
opinion that *York was neceffary to cover it, in
which cafe he might take York alfo*; and as the
two pofts might probably require more troops
than were intended to be left in Chefapeak, his
Lordfhip was at liberty to detain the whole *for
fortifying and garrifoning* them. I dare fay Lord
Cornwallis faw the order in this point of view;--
but judging that Old Point Comfort was totally
unfit for the purpofe defired, he had recourfe
to the inftructions and letters to General Phillips in his poffeffion, to fee whether they would
authorife him to reject it, and look out for
another. And difcovering that my inftructions
to that General officer gave him leave, "in
"cafe

"case the Admiral disapproving Portsmouth should require a fortified station for large ships in Chesapeak, and *should propose York town or Old Point Comfort*, to take possession thereof, if possession of either could be *acquired and maintained without great risk or loss*;" his Lordship conceived he should act according to the spirit of my orders, by taking York and Gloucester. I am however humbly of opinion, that admitting the propriety of his Lordship's consulting other papers besides the order immediately before him, the order (even as explained by the instructions) did not *become positive to occupy York and Gloucester*. For it does not appear that the instructions authorised either General Phillips or his Lordship to occupy York or Old Point Comfort, *unless they should have been proposed by the Admiral for a naval station*. But the post of York and Gloucester never having been proposed by the Admiral either to his Lordship or me for a naval station, as Old Point Comfort was, but only barely mentioned to his Lordship by the Admiral, as likely to command one of the principal rivers *if it could be secured*; and it at last appearing by the letter of 20th October, to have been his Lordship's

OBSERVATIONS. 29

Lordship's opinion that it was *incapable of being so*; it may be presumed that his Lordship did not act conformable to either the spirit or letter of the order in taking it, — and consequently that his *doing so was entirely of his own motion and choice*. But, being probably aware of this conclusion, his Lordship says, " as the harbour " was the indispensible object, he took York, " being the only one in Chesapeak that he knew " of." In which (no doubt) his Lordship would have been perfectly justifiable *if the objections to it were not such as he thought forcible*." But it appears from his Lordship's letter of the 20th of October, *that the objections to that post were such as he thought forcible*. It may therefore be a matter of some surprise, that, as his Lordship thought proper to avail himself of the *latitude of choice* he supposed given him by the instructions to General Phillips, it did not occur to him that the same instructions directed him to " *decline taking either York or Old Point* " *Comfort, if his objections were such as he* " *thought forcible*." And as Lord Cornwallis *never stated his objections to the post of York* either to the Admiral or me, as those instructions directed him to do, if he had any; it may be

asserted

asserted that his Lordship alone is answerable for whatever impropriety there may have been in *taking the post of York and Gloucester*; as it is I presume, clear from the foregoing reasoning, that, having under the sanction of the instructions to General Phillips, declined taking possession of *Old Point Comfort* (which his Lordship was positively directed to occupy by the order of the 11th of July,) his Lordship had *the same authority for declining to take York or any other naval station,* " could they not " be *acquired and maintained without great risk* " *or loss, and so well and so soon fortified as to be* " *rendered hors d' insulte before the enemy could* " *move a force, &c. against them*;"* which his Lordship's letter of the 20th of October intimates to be his opinion the post of York could not be *from the disadvantageous nature of the ground.*

Having represented to the minister for the American department the danger of operations in Chesapeak without a covering fleet; and having been in consequence promised that I should have it; and being told by Admiral

---

* Vide the instructions and substance of conversations with General Phillips, as quoted by Lord Cornwallis in his letter dated July 26, 1781.

ral Hood upon his arrival that he had brought me a sufficient one; I gave Lord Cornwallis of course all the hopes I could, and "*certain-ly promised to succour him in person, by moving into Chesapeak with four thousand troops,*" the instant the Admiral should inform me the passage to him was open, or would undertake to convoy me. But as his Lordship did not receive these hopes (such as they are) before the 16th of September; (for I must still persist in declaring that I never gave his Lordship *assurances of the exertions of the navy* before my letter to him of the 24th of September, which he received on the 29th — as asserted in his Lordship's letter of the 20th of October) Surely his Lordship's hopes of succour must have been but small between the 29th of August and that period, *when he knew there was an enemy's fleet of thirty-six sail of the line blocking him up, and a formidable army collecting to invest him,* " in an " intrenched camp, subject in most places to " enfilade, and the ground in general disad- " vantageous;"— without *knowing of more than seven sail of the line on our side,* and consequently having in the intermediate space no very great prospect of relief.

His

His Lordſhip ſays, " that, as I did not give " him the ſmalleſt particle of diſcretionary " power different from holding the poſts he " occupied; it would not have been juſtifiable " in him, either to abandon by the evacuation " of York a conſiderably quantity of artillery, " the ſhips of war, tranſports, proviſions, " ſtores, and hoſpitals; or, by venturing an " action without the moſt manifeſt advantage, " to run the riſk of precipitating the loſs of " them." To this, I ſhall only obſerve, that it will appear from the correſpondence, that his Lordſhip's diſcretionary powers were unlimited from the firſt moment of his taking charge of a ſeparate command; and it will I believe be admitted, that his Lordſhip acted in moſt caſes as if he conſidered them as ſuch. And though I may not condemn his Lordſhip for not attacking the Marquis de la Fayette, before his junction with Monſieur St. Simon (when he had, as I underſtand, only two thouſand regular continental troops); or for not attempting to prevent that junction; or for not attacking them when joined; and endeavouring to eſcape with part of his army to the ſouthward, between the 29th of Auguſt and the

16th

OBSERVATIONS.

16th of September; — as such measures must, have altogether depended on his Lordship's own feelings, of which no man can speak but himself. Yet it was natural to suppose, that the General officer, who had but a few months before (at the risk of engaging his Commander in Chief in operations, for which he could not be prepared; and perhaps at the risk of losing a valuable province under his immediate protection) decided upon a move with part of his army into Virginia, *" for urgent reasons," " being influenced thereto* (he says) *by the substance of a dispatch*, (he heard was coming to him,) without waiting to receive it, though it might have been expected in a few hours: — I say, it was natural to suppose, that the General officer who had done this, might have judged it equally expedient to decide upon retiring back again without waiting to receive *special discretionary* powers from his Commander in Chief, if he judged there was a great probability of his losing every thing, should he remain. Which, if it was so, I am bold to say, was a reason far more urgent for his endeavouring to save part of his army by any means in his power, than any his Lordship could

could suppose he had for quitting the Carolinas at the time he marched into Virginia.

There remains little more neceſſary in reply to Lord Cornwallis's introduction, but to obſerve, that the army and its followers in Virginia had been ſo increaſed in conſequence of his Lordſhip's move into that province; that it would have been impracticable to withdraw them by water (as his Lordſhip is pleaſed to ſuggeſt) for want of tranſports, even if the American miniſter had not directed me to ſupport his Lorſhip there, and a preſſing contingency had required it. And I muſt take the liberty to ſay, that the ſending his Lordſhip's corps back to South Carolina by land, would have been a moſt abſurd idea for me to adopt after the opinions I had given of the riſks it run in its former march by that route.

I ſhall now beg leave to conclude with an opinion, which I preſume is deducible from the foregoing (I truſt candid) review of circumſtances. Which is, that Lord Cornwallis's conduct and opinions, if they were not the immediate cauſes, may be adjudged to have at leaſt contributed to bring on the fatal cataſtrophe

trophe which terminated the unfortunate campaign of 1781.

H. CLINTON.

Harley- Street,
April 3, 1783.

APPENDIX.

PART I.

CONTAINING

EXTRACTS

FROM THE

Correspondence with Earl Cornwallis, respecting the Force left with his Lordship, and the Instructions given him upon his taking the Command of the Southern District.

Extract. — *From Sir Henry Clinton to Earl Cornwallis, dated Charles-town, May* 17, 1780.

YOUR Lordship has already with you, *(in the field)* two thousand five hundred and forty two rank and file; but, if you have the least reason to suppose the enemy likely to be in great number, you shall be reinforced with the forty-second, the light infantry, and any other corps you choose. As your move is important, it must not be stinted. — I will give you all you wish of every sort. —

Let me but know what it is as soon as possible. In the mean time, I shall order the light infantry and forty-second regiment to prepare; depending upon it, that as soon as you can spare them, you will return them to me; for all operations to the Northward must be cramped without them. If you choose to keep the seventeenth dragoons, you are heartily welcome to them during this move.

Copy.— From Earl Cornwallis to Sir Henry Clinton, dated Camp at Manigolds, May 18, 1780.

SIR,

LIEUTENANT Colonel Webster arrived this morning, and informed me of the message which you sent by him, relative to reinforcing the corps under my command. The service on which I am going, is undoubtedly of the most important nature, and in my opinion, without some success in the back country, our success at Charles-town would but little promote the real interests of Great-Britain. But at the same time it is as necessary that your situation to the Northward should be respectable. It would be with great regret that I should see you leave behind any part of that corps destined for your first embarkation. The garrison, then,

then, of Charles-town and Sullivan's-island, will confift of three Britifh regiments, — two of them very weak, — and two Heffian, and one weak Provincial, the latter of which, perhaps, will be fent to Fort Moultrie. This garrifon will have the charge of two thoufand five hundred prifoners. The corps at prefent under my command is, in my opinion, fully equal to the purpofe intended by it, unlefs fome confiderable reinforcement of Continentals fhould come from the Northward. I have not yet heard that fact afcertained, by any intelligence which has come to my knowledge. If troops are on their march, and not very near, your embarkation given out publicly for the Chefapeak will probably ftop them. I think, therefore, Sir, if you pleafe, with proper deference and fubmiffion to your opinion, that the bufinefs may be fettled in the following manner: If no certain intelligence arrives before you are ready to fail, of a confiderable corps of the Continental troops being far advanced, that the difpofition fhould then remain the fame which you mentioned when I had the honour of feeing you. If fuch intelligence fhould arrive before that time, I fhould then wifh to be joined by five or fix hundred men, either Britifh or Heffian, and fubmit it to your judgment on the fpot, from whence they could be beft fupplied. I think, at all events, Lieutenant-colonel Balfour's expedition fhould go on immediately, as the feafon of the year makes it neceſſary that he ſhould loſe no time. The more pains that can be taken to eſtabliſh the belief of your going to Virginia, the greater will be the probability of ſtopping their reinforcement.

   I am, &c.

    (Signed) CORNWALLIS.

Extract. — *From Earl Cornwallis to Sir Henry Clinton, dated Camp at Manigolds, May 19, 1780.*

 SIR,

I RECEIVED, very early this morning, the favour of your letter by Lieutenant-colonel Innes, to which the letter I had the honour of ſending to you yeſterday, by Major Danſey, will ſerve as an anſwer. I can only add, that I have received no intelligence whatever of reinforcements coming to the enemy from the Northward, or of their being in force in this province.

Extract.

Extract. — *From Sir Henry Clinton to Earl Cornwallis, dated Charles-town, May* 20, 1780.

———— THE light infantry and forty-second regiment march this evening to Goose-creek, and thence to Monk's-corner, where they will remain at your Lordship's call, in readiness either to join you, or to return and embark, as shall have become expedient.

Extract. — *From Sir Henry Clinton to Earl Cornwallis, dated Charles-town, May* 20, 1780.

EVERY jealousy has been and will be given on my part, as a blind to our real intentions.

And now, my Lord, having entered into every thing that occurs to me as necessary to be thought on at present, I heartily wish success to your important move. I cannot doubt your having it, for as much as I agree with you, that success at Charles-town, unless followed in the back country, will be of little avail; so much, I am persuaded, that the taking that place in the advantageous manner we have done it, insures the reduction of this and the next province, if the temper of our friends in those districts is such as it has always been represented to us.

Extract.

Extract. — *From Earl Cornwallis to Sir Henry Clinton, dated Camp at Lenews, East Side of Santée, May* 21, 1780.

THE march of the light infantry and forty-second to Monk's-corner will be of use to those corps, and will help to spread alarm through the country; but from what I hear, I do not believe that there can be any necessity for detaining any part of the first embarkation a moment after the ships are ready for them.

Extract. — *Sir Henry Clinton to Earl Cornwallis, dated Charles-Town, June* 1, 1780.

WE shall probably leave this in a day or two. — I dare not be so sanguine as to suppose that your business will be compleated in time for us to meet before I sail; and as our communication will become precarious, I think it necessary to give your Lordship outlines of my intentions, where your Lordship is likely to bear a part. Your Lordship knows it was part of my plan to have gone into Chesapeak bay; but I am apprehensive the information which the Admiral and I received, may make it necessary for him to assemble his fleet at New-York,

in

—in which case I shall go there likewise. When your Lordship has finished your campaign, you will be better able to judge what is necessary to be done to secure South and recover North Carolina. Perhaps it may be necessary to send the gallies and some troops into Cape Fear, to awe the lower counties, by far the most hostile of that province, and to prevent the conveyance of succours by inland navigation, the only communication that will probably remain with the northern parts of North Carolina and Virginia. Should your Lordship so far succeed in both provinces, as to be satisfied they are safe from any attack during the approaching season, after leaving a sufficient force in garrison, and such other posts as you think necessary, and such troops by way of moving corps as you shall think sufficient, added to such provincial and militia corps as you shall judge proper to raise; I should wish you to assist in operations which will certainly be carried on in the Chesapeak, as soon as we are relieved from our apprehension of a superior fleet, and the season will admit of it in that climate. This may happen, perhaps, about September, or, if not, early in October. I am clear this should not be atttempted without a great naval force; — I am not so clear there should be a great land force. I therefore propose that your Lordship, with what you can spare at the time from your important post, *(which is always to be considered as the principal object)* may meet the Admiral, who

who will bring with him such additional force as I can spare into the Chesapeak. I should recommend in the first place, that one or two armed ships, vigilants, should be prepared, and that as many gallies as can go to sea may likewise accompany you from hence. Our first object will probably be the taking post at Norfolk or Suffolk, *or near the Hampton Road,* and then proceeding up the Chesapeak to *Baltimore.* I shall not presume to say any thing by way of instruction to your Lordship, except in articles where you wish it; and if you will do me the honour to inform me of your wishes by the first safe opportunity, I shall pay every attention to them upon that subject, or any other. The Admiral assures me that there will be ships enough left for convoy, ready by the 24th of June. Your Lordship will be the best judge what use can be made of them. Correspondence may, and I hope will, be kept up by the cruizers, which the Admiral and officer stationed here will have, but if you find it necessary, you will be so good to press or hire armed vessels.

Extract. — From Instructions to Lieutenant General Earl Cornwallis, dated Head-Quarters, Charlestown, June 1, 1780.

UPON my departure from hence, you will be pleased to take command of the troops mentioned in
the

the inclosed return, and of all other troops now here, or that may arrive in my absence. Your Lordship will make such change in the position of them, as you may judge most conducive to his Majesty's service, for the defence of this important post, and its dependencies. At the same time, it is by no means my intention to prevent your acting offensively, in case an opportunity should offer, consistent with the *security of this place*, which is always to be regarded as *a primary object*.

All provision and military stores of any denomination now here, or which may hereafter arrive, are submitted to your Lordship's orders, together with every power you may find necessary to enforce in my absence, for the promotion of the King's service.

Extract.—*From Sir Henry Clinton to Earl Cornwalllis, dated Romulus, June* 8, 1780.

MY LORD,

I HAVE the honour to transmit to your Lordship the names of several inhabitants of the town, who signed an address, the copy of which Brigadier-general Paterson will send you. Inclosed is a copy of the answer the Admiral proposed sending until I represented to him that the subscribers were unknown

known to us as to their several characters; that the superintendant was not with us to be consulted; that the permitting exportation amounted to opening the port, which we were not empowered to do; and that I would, reluctantly, at the hour of my departure, change, within your Lordship's command, the conditions of so many persons, without knowing their merits. I also considered that property, in the late troubles, might have been very unwarrantably acquired, and that exportation realized it to the present possessors.

In consequence, the inclosed answer was substituted, bettering their present condition, and opening the prospect of trade, and the restoration of civil government.

To this, my Lord, I have to add, in the Admiral's and my own name, that you are empowered still farther to indulge men who exhibit proofs of a sincere return to their duty, by admitting them to any greater degree of liberty, to the fullest enjoyment of their property, and to the permission, in particular cases, of shipping it, when the officer commanding the King's ships shall furnish convoy; all which advantages I will ratify either as Commissioner or Commander-in-chief.

PART II.

PART II.

CONTAINING

Copies and Extracts from Letters, relative to the entire Submission of South Carolina, and the progressive Operations proposed in Consequence, for the Reduction of North Carolina.

Extract. — *From Earl Cornwallis to Sir Henry Clinton, dated Charles-town, June 30, 1780.*

——THE submission of General Williamson at Ninety-Six, whose capitulation I inclose with Captain Paris's letter; and the dispersion of a party of rebels, who had assembled at an Iron-work, on the north west border of the province, by a detachment of dragoons and militia, from Lieutenant-colonel Turnbull, put an end to all resistance in South Carolina.

FROM THE SAME.

THE force of the enemy in North Carolina confists of about one hundred militia at Crofs-Creek, under General Cafwell; four or five hundred militia, at or near Salifbury, under General Rutherford; and three hundred Virginians in that neighbourhood, under one Porterfield.

———— returned with information that he faw two thoufand Maryland and Delaware troops at Hillfborough under Major-general De Calbe. Other accounts correfponded with his. But I have fince heard that the greateft part of the laft have returned to Virginia.

After having thus fully ftated the prefent fituation of the two Carolinas, I fhall now take the liberty of giving my opinion, with refpect to the practicability and the probable effect of farther operations in this quarter, and my own intentions, if not otherwife directed by your Excellency. I think, that with the force at prefent under my command (except there fhould be a confiderable *foreign* interference) I can leave South Carolina in fecurity, and march about the beginning of September, with a body of troops, into the back part of North Carolina, with the greateft probability of reducing that province to its duty. And if this be accomplifhed, I am of opinion, that (befides the advantage of poffeffing fo valuable a province)

vince) it would prove an effectual barrier for South Carolina and Georgia; and could be kept, with the assistance of our friends there, by as few troops as would be wanted on the borders of this province, if North Carolina should remain in the hands of our enemies. Consequently, if your Excellency should continue to think it expedient to employ part of the troops at present in this province, in operations in the Chesapeak, there will be as many to spare, as if we did not possess North Carolina. If I am not honoured with different directions from your Excellency before that time, I shall take my measures for beginning the execution of the above plan about the latter end of August, or beginning of September, and shall apply to the officer commanding his Majesty's ships for some co-operation, by Cape Fear, which at present would be burthensome to the navy, and not of much importance to the service.

Extract. — *From Earl Cornwallis to Sir Henry Clinton, dated Charles-town, July, 14, 1780.*

I HAVE the satisfaction to assure your Excellency, that the numbers and dispositions of our militia, equal my most sanguine expectations. But still I must confess, that their want of subordination and confi-

confidence in themselves, will make a considerable regular force always neceffary for the defence of the province, until North Carolina is perfectly reduced. It will be needlefs to attempt to take any confiderable number of the South Carolina militia with us, when we advance. They can only be looked upon as light troops, and we fhall find friends enough in the next province of the fame quality; and we muft not undertake to fupply too many ufelefs mouths.

Extract. — From Earl Cornwallis to Sir Henry Clinton, dated Charles-town, Aug. 6, 1780.

SIR,

I RECEIVED by Major England, your letters of the 14th and 15th of July; and am very glad to find by the latter, that you do not place much dependance on receiving troops from hence.

My letter of the 14th, by the Halifax, will have convinced you of the impoffibility of weakening the force in this province; and every thing which has happened fince that time, tends more ftrongly to confirm it. The general ftate of things in the two provinces of North and South Carolina, is not very materially altered fince my letters of the 14th and 15th of laft month were written. Frequent fkirmifhes, skirmishes, with various success, have happened in the country between the Catawba-river and Broad-river. The militia of the district about Tiger and Ennoree rivers, was formed by us, under a Colonel Floyd; Colonel Neale, the rebel colonel, had fled; but Lieutenant-colonel Lisle, who had been paroled to the islands, exchanged, on his arrival in Charles-town, his parole for a certificate of his being a good subject, returned to the country, and carried off the whole battalion to join General Sumpter, at Catawba. We have not, however, on the whole, lost ground in that part of the country. Turnbull was attacked at Rocky-mount, by Sumpter, with about twelve hundred men, militia and refugees, from this province, whom he repulsed with great loss. We had on our part, an officer killed, and one wounded, and about ten or twelve men killed and wounded. Colonel Turnbull's conduct was very meritorious. The affair of Captain Huck turned out of less consequence than it appeared at first; the Captain and three men of the legion were killed, and seven men of the New-York volunteers taken.

On the eastern part of the province, we have been more unfortunate. By this time the reports industriously propagated in this province, of a large army coming from the northward, had very much intimidated our friends, encouraged our enemies, and determined the wavering against us; to which
our

our not advancing and acting offensively likewise contributed.

The whole country between Pedée and Santée has ever since been in an absolute state of rebellion; every friend of Government has been carried off, and his plantation destroyed; and detachments of the enemy have appeared on the Santée, and threatened our stores and convoys on that river. I have not heard that they have as yet made any attempt on them; and I hope, by this time, the steps I have taken will secure them. This unfortuate business, if it should have no worse consequences, will shake the confidence of our friends in this province, and make our situation very uneasy until we can advance. The wheat harvest in North Carolina is now over, but the weather is still excessively hot, and notwithstanding our utmost exertions, a great part of the rum, salt, clothing, and necessaries for the soldiers, and the arms for the Provincials and ammunition for the troops, are not far advanced on their way to Camden. However, if no material interruption happens, this business will be nearly accomplished in a fortnight or three weeks. It may be doubted by some, whether the invasion of North Carolina may be a prudent measure; but I am convinced it is a necessary one, and that if we do not attack that province, we must give up both South Carolina and Georgia, and retire within the walls of Charles-town. Our assurances of attachment

ment from our poor diſtreſſed friends in North Carolina are as ſtrong as ever, and the patience and fortitude with which thoſe unhappy people bear the moſt oppreſſive and cruel tyranny, that ever was exerciſed over any country, deſerve our greateſt admiration. The Highlanders have offered to form a regiment as ſoon as we enter the country, and have deſired that Governor Martin may be their chief. I have conſented with the rank of Lieutenant-colonel commandant; the men they aſſure us are already engaged.

An early diverſion in my favour in Cheſapeak Bay, will be of the greateſt and moſt important advantage to my operations. I moſt earneſtly hope that the admiral will be able to ſpare a convoy for that purpoſe.

I propoſe taking the following corps with me into North Carolina, twenty-third, thirty-third, ſixty-third, ſeventy-firſt, volunteers of Ireland, Hamilton's, Harriſon's, new-raiſed, legion cavalry, and infantry, North Carolina refugees. I intend to leave on the frontiers, from Pedée to Waxhaw (to awe the diſſaffected, who, I am ſorry to ſay, are ſtill very numerous in that country, and to prevent any inſurrection in our rear) the New York volunteers, and Brown's corps, and ſome of the militia of the Camden diſtrict, who are commanded by Colonel Rugely, a very active and ſpirited man. I ſhall place Ferguſon's corps and ſome militia of the Ninety-ſix diſtrict,

which

which Colonel Balfour assures me are got into very tolerable order, owing to the great assiduity of Ferguson, on the borders of Tryon county, with directions for him to advance with a part of them into the mountains, and secure the left of our march. Lieutenant-colonel Cruger, who commands at Ninety-six, will have his own corps, Innes's and the remainder of the militia of that district, to preserve that frontier, which requires great attention, and where there are many disaffected, and many constantly in arms. Allen's corps, and for a time, the Florida rangers, are stationed at Augusta, under the command of Lieutenant-colonel Allen.

——— I have already explained the measures I had taken for establishing a government, and securing this country by means of a militia. I have likewise paid as much attention as possible to the civil and commercial matters. The principal objects of my attention will appear in the five proclamations, which I have issued, and which I have the honour of inclosing to your Excellency.

I have the honour, &c.

(Signed)   CORNWALLIS.

PAT III.

PART III.

CONTAINING

EXTRACTS

FROM THE

Correspondence with Earl Cornwallis, respecting the Events which occurred between the Battle of Camden and Major Ferguson's Defeat.

Extract. — *From Earl Cornwallis to Sir Henry Clinton, dated Camden, August* 23, 1780.

I HAVE not yet heard any accounts from North Carolina; but I hope that our friends will immediately take arms, as I have directed them to do. The diversion in the Chesapeak will be of the utmost importance. The troops here have gained reputation, but they have lost numbers; and there can be no doubt but the enemy will use every effort to repel an attack, which, if succesful, must end in their losing all the Southern Colonies.

I have likewise to observe, that if a general exchange should take place, the enemy's prisoners should, in my opinion, be delivered at the same place as ours are sent to.

It is difficult to form a plan of operations, which must depend so much on circumstances. But it at present appears to me that I should endeavour to get as soon as possible to Hillsborough, and there assemble and try to arrange the friends who are inclined to arm in our favour; and endeavour to form a very large magazine for the winter, of flour and meal from the country; and of rum, salt, &c. from Cross-creek, which I understand to be about eighty miles carriage. But all this will depend on the operations which your Excellency may think proper to pursue in the Chesapeak, which appears to me next to the security of New-York, to be one of the most important objects of the war. I can only repeat what I have often had the honour of saying to you, that wherever you may think my presence can be most conducive to the good of his Majesty's service, thither I am at all times ready and willing to go.

Extract. — From Earl Cornwallis to Lord George Germain, dated Camden, August 20, 1780.

IN the district of ninety-six, by far the most populous and powerful of the province, Lieutenant-colonel Balfour by his great attention and diligence, and by the active assistance of Major Ferguson, who was appointed Inspector-general of militia of this province by Sir Henry Clinton, had formed seven battalions of militia, consisting of above four thousand men, and entirely composed of persons well-affected

affected to the British Government; which were so regulated that they could with ease furnish fifteen hundred men at a short notice, for the defence of the frontier, or any other home service. But I must take this opportunity of observing, that this militia can be of little use for distant operations, as they will not stir without a horse, and on that account your Lordship will easily conceive the impossibility of keeping a number of them together without destroying the country.

Extract. — From Earl Cornwallis to Lord George Germain, dated Camden, August 21, 1780.

ON the morning of the 17th I dispatched proper people into North-Carolina, with directions to our friends there to take arms and assemble immediately; and to seize the most violent people and all military stores and magazines belonging to the rebels, and to intercept all stragglers from the routed army. And I have promised to march without loss of time to their support. Some necessary supplies for the army are now on their way from Charles-town; and I hope that their arrival will enable me to move in a few days.

Extract. — From Earl Cornwallis to Sir Henry Clinton, dated Camden, August 29, 1780.

I HOPE to be able to move my first division in eight or nine days into North Carolina by Charlotte-town

town and Salisbury; the second will follow in about ten days after, with convalescents and stores. I shall leave the New York volunteers and Innes's corps to take care of this place until the sick and stores can be removed. Our sickness at present is rather at a stand, the recoveries nearly keeping pace with the falling down. I dread the convalescents not being able to march; but it is very tempting to try it, as a move of forty or fifty miles would put us into a much better climate.

Ferguson is to move into Tryon County with some militia, whom he says he is sure *he can depend upon for doing their duty and fighting well;* but I am sorry to say that his own experience as well as that of every other officer is against him.

I most sincerely hope that nothing can happen to prevent your Excellency's intended diversion in the Chesapeak. If unfortunately any unforeseen cause should make it impossible, I should hope that you will see the absolute necessity of adding some force to the Carolinas.

Extract.—From Sir Henry Clinton to Earl Cornwallis, dated New-York, September 20, 1780.

I HAVE always thought operation in the Chesapeak of the greatest importance, and have often mentioned to Admiral Arbuthnot the necessity of making a diversion in your Lordship's favour in that quarter

quarter; but have not been able till now to obtain a convoy for this purpose.

Your Lordship will receive inclosed a sketch of the instructions I intend to give to Major-general Leslie, who will command the expedition; which will give a general idea of the design of the move. But if your Lordship should wish any particular co-operation from that armament, General Leslie will of course consider himself under your Lordship's orders, and pay every obedience thereto.

I have the honour to inclose the copy of a letter I wrote to Lord George Germain, and of his Lordship's answer, respecting the option Lord Rawdon had made in favour of his provincial rank. And I am happy in having it in my power to communicate to his Lordship the King's pleasure that he should still retain his rank of Lieutenant-colonel in the line, which I beg leave to take this opportunity of doing through your Lordship.

INCLOSURES.

Copy.—*Sir Henry Clinton to Lord George Germain, dated Charles-Town, June 3, 1780.*

MY LORD,

LORD Rawdon, in consequence of his Majesty's order signified to me by your Lordship, has resigned his commission of Lieutenant-colonel in the army, and made choice of that of Colonel of Provincias

In

In juftice to his Lordfhip, as well as to the King's fervice, I muft obferve that the expences Lord Rawdon has been at, and the diftinguifhed zeal he has fhewn in forming the corps under his command, render him worthy of much commendation, and make the alternative put to him a very mortifying one; whilft on the other hand, the volunteers of Ireland; bereft of a chief of his Lordfhip's rank in life, and attention to the fervice, would probably have loft much in their ftrength and difcipline.

Perhaps his Majefty may be gracioufly pleafed to confider his Lordfhip in the light of an officer, who, for the good of his fervice and the prefervation of a ferviceable corps, to which he felt a kind of parental attachment, has offered to relinquifh rank effential to his future hopes as a foldier; and may, in confequence, reftore to him his brevet of Lieutenant-colonel in the army.

I have the honour, &c.

H. CLINTON.

Extract. — *From Lord G. Germain to Sir H. Clinton, dated Whitehall, July 5,* 1780.

You will find by my feparate letter of yefterday, that it is not his Majefty's intention to confine you to fo ftrict an obfervance of the general rule of no officers being permitted to hold commiffions in a regular and provincial corps at the fame time, as to prevent

prevent you from deviating from it in extraordinary cases; and that your having done so in favour of Majors Simcoe and Tarleton, was approved by his Majesty. I also informed you, that the general rule was not meant to affect the brevet rank of officers. It is therefore a great concern to me to find Lord Rawdon had resigned his rank of Lieutenant-colonel in the army, when he made his option of Colonel of the Provincials. The King is fully sensible of his Lordship's merit, and of the great advantage which the corps under his command has derived from his Lordship's attention to it; and is well pleased his Lordship has chosen to continue at the head of it. But his Majesty commands me to signify to you his royal pleasure, that you do immediately acquaint his Lordship, that he still retains his rank of Lieutenant-colonel in the army.

Instructions to the Hon. Major-general Leslie, dated Head-Quarters, New-York, October 10, 1780.

SIR,

YOU will be pleased to proceed with the troops embarked under your command to Chesapeak Bay; and upon your arrival at that place, you will pursue such measures as you shall judge most likely to answer the purpose of this expedition, the principal object of which is to make a diversion in favour of Lieutenant-general Earl Cornwallis, who by the time you arrive there will probably be acting in the back parts of North Carolina. The information you shall procure

cure on the spot after your arrival at your destined port, will point out to you the properest method of accomplishing this. But from that which I have received here, I should judge it best to proceed up James River as high as possible, in order to seize or destroy any magazines the enemy may have at Petersburg, Richmond, or any of the places adjacent; and finally, to establish a post on Elizabeth River. But this, as well as the direction of every other operation, is submitted to Earl Cornwallis, with whom you are as soon as possible to communicate, and afterwards to follow all such orders and directions you shall from time to time receive from his Lordship.

H. CLINTON.

Extract,—Sir Henry Clinton to Earl Cornwallis, dated New-York, November 6, 1780.

YOUR Lordship can judge of the strength of this part of the army, by that under your own orders; and will agree with me that it is scarcely possible for me to detach a greater force from it, or of our being able to make such efforts in Chesapeak Bay, as are now almost become necessary. However, when I know your Lordship's success in North Carolina, and your determination respecting a post on Elizabeth River, I will then consider what additional force I can spare. If your Lordship determines to withdraw that post, I shall in that case think your present force, including General Leslie's, quite sufficient.

By the copy of inſtructions laſt ſent, and thoſe now forwarded to General Leſlie, your Lordſhip will perceive I mean that you ſhould take the command of the whole. If my wiſhes are fulfilled, they are, that you may *eſtabliſh a poſt at Hillſborough, feed it from Croſs Creek, and be able to keep that of Portſmouth.* A few troops will do it, and carry on deſultory expeditions in Cheſapeak, *till more ſolid operations can take place;—of which I fear* there is no proſpect, without we are conſiderably reinforced. The moment I know your Lordſhip's determination to keep a poſt at Portſmouth, I will, as I ſaid before, conſider what additional force I can ſpare. *Once aſſured of our remaining ſuperior at ſea,* I might poſſibly ſend two thouſand more for this winter's operations.

Operations in Cheſapeak are but of two ſorts. Solid operation with a fighting army, to call forth our friends and ſupport them; or a poſt, ſuch as Portſmouth, carrying on deſultory expeditions; ſtopping up in a great meaſure the Cheſapeak; and by commanding James River, prevent the enemy from forming any conſiderable depots upon it, or moving in any force to the ſouthward of it. Such, my Lord, are the advantages I expect from a ſtation at Portſmouth; and I wiſh it may appear to you in the ſame light.

Second Inſtructions to the Hon. Major-general Leſlie, dated New-York, November 2, 1780.

SIR,

HAVING already put you under the orders of
Lord

Lord Cornwallis, who muſt of courſe be the beſt judge of operations to the ſouthward, it may be needleſs to ſay any thing more. But leſt you ſhould not receive any orders from his Lordſhip, or obtain certain intelligence relative to him; or have reaſon to ſuppoſe you can better aſſiſt his operations by a diverſion made nearer him; I think it neceſſary to give you ſome hints reſpecting Cape Fear River, and how far the acting upon that river may operate. Should Lord Cornwallis have paſſed the Yadkin, and be advanced towards Hillſborough, I think you cannot act any where ſo well as on James River, approaching ſometimes towards the Roanoke, but not paſſing that river without orders from Lord Cornwallis. If you have every reaſon to believe that his Lordſhip meets with oppoſition at his paſſage of the Yadkin, I think a move on Cape Fear River will operate effectually. I have had much converſation with General O'Hara on this ſubject. I have given him every information reſpecting that move; and I truſt after conſulting him you will act in the beſt manner poſſible to fulfill the object of all your inſtructions — *a diverſion in favour of Lord Cornwallis.* That you may be the better judge of his plan, I ſend you copies of ſuch of his letters, which give any hints towards it.

You will of courſe cautiouſly avoid inrolling any of the militia of Princeſs Anne or elſewhere, without you on determine to eſtabliſh a poſt. Thoſe, however, who voluntarily join you muſt be taken care of.

H. CLINTON.
Extract.

Extract. — From *Earl Cornwallis* to *Sir Henry Clinton*, dated Camp at *Waxhaw*, September 22, 1780.

IF nothing material happens to obstruct my plan of operations, I mean, as soon as Lieutenant-colonel Tarleton can be removed, to proceed with the twenty-third, thirty-third, volunteers of Ireland, and Legion, to Charlotte-town, and leave the seventy-first here until the sick can be brought on to us. I then mean to make some redoubts and establish a fixed post at that place, and give the command of it to Major Wimys, whose regiment is so totally demolished by sickness, that it will not be fit for actual service for some months. To that place I shall bring up all the sick from Camden, who have any chance of being serviceable before Christmas, and trust to opportunities for their joining the army.

The post at Charlotte-town will be a great security to all this frontier of South-Carolina, which, even if we were possessed of the greatest part of North-Carolina, would be liable to be infested by parties, who have retired with their effects over the mountains, and mean to take every opportunity of carrying on a predatory war, and it will, I hope, prevent insurrections in this country, which is very disaffected. I then think of moving on my principal force to Salisbury, which will open this country sufficiently for us to see what assistance we may really expect from our friends in North-Carolina; and will give us a

free

free communication with the Highlanders, on whom my greatest dependance is placed.

Extract. — From Earl Cornwallis to Lord George Germain, dated Camp at Waxhaw, September 19, 1780.

MY LORD,

I HAD the honour to inform your Lordship in my letter of the 21st of August, that I had dispatched proper people into North-Carolina to exhort our friends in that province to take arms, to seize military stores, and magazines of the enemy, and to intercept all stragglers of the routed army.

Some parties of our friends, who had embodied themselves near the Pedée, disarmed several of the enemy's stragglers. But the leading persons of the Loyalists were so undecided in their councils, that they lost the critical time of availing themselves of our success; and even suffered General Gates to pass to Hillsborough with a guard of six men only. They continue however to give me the strongest assurances of support, when his Majesty's troops shall have penetrated into the interior parts of the province. The patience and fortitude with which they endure the most cruel torments, and suffer the most violent oppressions that a country ever laboured under, convince me that they are sincere, at least as far as their affection, to the cause of Great-Britain.

PART IV.

CONTAINING

EXTRACTS

FROM THE

Correspondence with Earl Cornwallis, &c. from Major Ferguson's Misfortune to his Lordship's second Move into North Carolina.

Extract. — From Major-general Leslie to Sir Henry Clinton, dated Portsmouth, Nov. 7, 1780, eight at Night.

SIR,

THIS instant Lieutenant Gratton, of the sixty-fourth, is arrived express from Charles-town, in his Majesty's ship Iris, with a letter from Lord Rawdon, Lord Cornwallis being a little indisposed.

I inclose your Excellency a copy of the contents. I called on Commodore Gayton, and Brigadier-general Howard, for their opinion how we should act. We all agree to go to Cape Fear as soon as possible. Very sorry it is necessary; but my orders from your

Excellency is to co-operate and act with his Lordship to the utmost of my power.

Copy. — From Lord Rawdon to Major-general Leslie, dated Camp, near the Indian Lands, West of Cattawba river, South Carolina, Oct. 24, 1780.

SIR,

LORD Cornwallis not being sufficiently recovered from a severe fever which lately attacked him to be able to write to you, his Lordship has desired that I should have the honour of communicating with you upon the subject of the present service. The Commander in Chief has transmitted to Lord Cornwallis a copy of the instructions under which you are to act. At the time when Petersburgh was suggested as an adviseable point for a diversion, which might co-operate with our intended efforts for the reduction of North Carolina, it was imagined that the tranquillity of South Carolina was assured; and the repeated assurances which were sent to us by the Loyalists in North Carolina, gave us reason to hope, that their number and their zeal would not only facilitate the restoration of his Majesty's government in that province, but might also supply a force for more extensive operations. Events unfortunately have not answered to these flattering promises. The appearance of General Gates's army unveiled to us a fund of difaffection in this province, of which we could have formed no idea; and even the difperfion of that force did not extinguifh the ferment which the hope of its fupport had raifed. This hour the majority of the inhabitants of that tract between the Pedee and the Santée are in arms againft us; and when we laft heard from Charles-town, they were in poffeffion of George-town, from which they had diflodged our militia.

It was hoped that the rifing which was expected of our friends in North Carolina might awe that diftrict into quiet; therefore, after giving them a little chaftifement, by making the feventh regiment take that route in its way to the army, Lord Cornwallis advanced to Charlotteburg.

Major Ferguson, with about eight hundred militia collected from the neighbourhood of Ninety-fix, had previoufly marched into Tryon county to protect our friends, who were fuppofed to be numerous there; and it was intended, that he fhould crofs the Cattawba river, and endeavour to preferve tranquillity in the rear of the army. A numerous army now appeared on the frontiers, drawn from Nolachucki, and other fettlements beyond the mountains, whofe very names had been unknown to us. A body of thefe, joined by the inhabitants of the ceded lands in Georgia, made a fudden and violent attack upon Augufta. The poft was gallantly defended by Lieutenant-colonel

nel Brown, till he was relieved by the activity of Lieutenant-colonel Cruger: but Major Ferguson, by endeavouring to intercept the enemy in their retreat, unfortunately gave time for fresh bodies of men to pass the mountains, and to unite into a corps far superior to that which he commanded. They came up with him, and after a sharp action entirely defeated him. Ferguson was killed, and all his party either slain or taken.

By the enemy's having secured all the passes on the Cattawba, Lord Cornwallis (who was waiting at Charlotteburg for a convoy of stores) received but confused accounts of the affair for some time: but at length the truth reached him; and the delay, equally with the precautions the enemy had taken to keep their victory from his knowledge, gave Lord Cornwallis great reason to fear for the safety of Ninety-six. To secure that district was indispensible for the security of the rest of the province; and Lord Cornwallis saw no means of effecting it, but by passing the Cattawba river with his army; for it was so weakened by sickness, that it would not bear detachment.

After much fatigue on the march, occasioned by violent rains, we passed the river three days ago. We then received the first intelligence, respecting the different posts in this province, which had reached us for near three weeks; every express from Camden having been waylaid, and some of them murdered by the inhabitants. — Ninety-six is safe: the corps which

which defeated Ferguson having, in consequence of our movement, crossed the Cattawba, and joined Smallwood on the Yadkin.

In our present position we have received the first intimation of the expedition under your command. From the circumstances which I have detailed, we fear that we are too far asunder to render your co-operation very effectual. No force has presented itself to us, whose operation could have been thought serious against this army: but then we have little hopes of bringing the affair to the issue of an action. The enemy are mostly mounted militia, not to be overtaken by our infantry, nor to be safely pursued in this strong country by our cavalry. Our fear is, that instead of meeting us, they would slip by us into this province, were we to proceed far from it, and might again stimulate the disaffected to serious insurrection. This apprehension you will judge, Sir, must greatly circumscribe our efforts. Indeed, Lord Cornwallis cannot hope that he shall be able to undertake any thing upon such a scale, as either to aid you, or to benefit from you in our present situation. The Commander in Chief has signified to Lord Cornwallis, that his Lordship is at liberty to give you any direction for farther co-operation which may appear to him expedient. But his Excellency has complied so very fully and completely with Lord Cornwallis's request, by sending so powerful a force to make a diversion in the Chesapeak, that his Lordship fears

he

he should require too much, were he to draw you into the immediate service of this district. His Lordship is likewise delicate on this point, because he does not know how far, by drawing you from the Chesapeak, he might interfere with any other purposes to which the Commander in Chief may have destined your troops. Under these circumstances, Lord Cornwallis thinks himself obliged to leave you at liberty to pursue whatever measures may appear to your judgment best for his Majesty's service, and most consonant with the wishes of the Commander in Chief. No time is specified to Lord Cornwallis as the limitation of your stay to the southward. Should your knowledge of Sir Henry Clinton's desires prompt you to make a trial upon North Carolina, Cape Fear river appears to us to be the only part where your efforts are at present likely to be effectual. A descent there would be the surest means of joining and arming the friends of government, as well as of co-operating with this army.

This, therefore, would naturally be the point to which Lord Cornwallis would bring you, did he conceive himself at liberty so absolutely to dispose of you. It must be remarked, however, that there are two difficulties in this plan; the first is, that the country from Cape Fear to Cross-creek (the Highland settlement) produces so little, it would be requisite in penetrating through it to carry your provisions with you; the second is, that no vessel larger

than

than a frigate can pass the bar of Cape Fear harbour. Whatever you decide, Lord Cornwallis desires earnestly to hear from you as soon as possible.

'Tis uncertain yet what steps this army (if left to itself) must pursue; but it will be ready at least to act vigorously in aid to any plan which you may undertake. Lord Cornwallis begs that you will inform the Commander in Chief of our circumstances, and that you will have the goodness to mention how highly sensible his Lordship is to the very effectual manner in which his Excellency has endeavoured to ease the operations of his army. The measure must have been attended with the most favourable consequences, had not accidents, which no foresight could expect, so greatly altered the complexion of our affairs in this province.

Lord Cornwallis desires me to add how much satisfaction he should feel in having your assistance upon this service, did it promise more favourably for you. But should the intentions of the Commander in Chief have left you at liberty to make the attempt at Cape Fear, the success which would probably attend that essential service would be doubly pleasing to Lord Cornwallis, from the opportunity it would most likely give him of congratulating you in person. Allow me to add my hopes that the course of the service would put it in my power to assure you, personally, how much

I have the honour to be, &c.

(Signed) RAWDON.

Copy

Extracts of Letters previous to the

Copy.—*From Sir Henry Clinton, to Major-General Leslie, dated New-York, November* 12, 1780.

SIR,

I have this morning received your dispatches, and by that dated the 7th instant, I observe your intention of quitting the Chesapeak; and at the requisition of Earl Cornwallis, made to you in a letter written by Lord Rawdon, that you propose going to Cape Fear River with the force under your command. I entirely approve of your having obeyed Earl Cornwallis's directions and desire on this subject, which I hope will be attended with every favourable advantage.

It is not necessary for me to enter upon the matter of your operations in the Chesapeak, as they will now cease.

I have the honour, &c.

(Signed) H. CLINTON.

Extract.—*From Major-General Leslie to Sir Henry Clinton, on* board the Romulus, *dated Hampton Road, November* 19, 1780.

THE people in general seem sorry at our leaving this district, and I believe would have been happy to have remained quiet at home. It is a plentiful

country

country all round our posts; from my first hearing of Ferguson's fate, I inwardly suspected what came to pass; therefore I never issued any proclamation of my *own*, nor did I encourage the people to take arms. Many blamed me for it, but now they think I acted right.

I left the works entire, and I still hope that you will be able to take up this ground; for it certainly is the key to the wealth of Virginia and Maryland. It is to be lamented we are so weak in ships of war, for there is a fleet of sixty sail expected hourly from the West Indies, besides the valuable ships or craft ready to sail from the Chesapeak.

Copy.—From Lord Rawdon to Sir Henry Clinton, camp between Broad River and the Catawba, dated October 29, 1780.

SIR,

LORD Cornwallis having been so reduced by a severe fever, as to be still unable to write, he has desired that I should have the honour of addressing your Excellency in regard to our present situation. But few days have past since Lord Carnwallis received your Excellency's dispatch of the 20th of September. In consequence of it, his Lordship directed that I should immediately send a letter to meet Major-General Leslie in the Chesapeak;

giving

giving him the fullest information respecting our prospects, and the present temper of the country, I have the honour to inclose a copy of that letter. Something remains to be said in addition to it, of a nature which Earl Cornwallis judged inexpedient to unveil, excepting to your Excellency.

For some time after the arrival of his Majesty's troops at Camden, repeated messages were sent to head quarters, by the friends of government in North Carolina, expressing their impatience to rise and join the King's standard. The impossibility of subsisting that additional force at Camden, and the accounts which they themselves gave of the distressing scarcity, of provisions in North Carolina, obliged Lord Cornwallis to entreat them to remain quiet, till the new crop might enable us to join them. In the mean time General Gates's army advanced. We were greatly surprised, and no less grieved, that no information whatever of its movements was conveyed to us by persons so deeply interested in the event as the North Carolina Loyalists. Upon the 16th of August that army was so entirely dispersed, that it was clear no number of them could for a considerable time be collected. Orders were therefore dispatched to our friends, stating that the hour, which they had so long pressed, was arrived; and exhorting them to stand forth immediately, and prevent the re-union of the scattered enemy. Instant support was in that case promised them. In the fullest confidence that this

event

event was to take place, Lord Cornwallis ventured to press your Excellency for co-operation in the Chesapeak, hoping that the affiftance of the North Carolinians might eventually furnifh a force for yet farther efforts. Not a fingle man, however, attempted to improve the favourable moment, or obeyed that fummons for which they had before been fo impatient. It was hoped that our approach might get the better of their timidity ; yet during a long period, whilft we were waiting at Charlotteburgh for our ftores and convalefcents, they did not even furnifh us with the leaft information refpecting the force collecting againft us. In fhort, Sir, we may have a powerful body of friends in North Carolina, — and indeed we have caufe to be convinced, that many of the inhabitants wifh well to his Majefty's arms ; but they have not given evidence enough either of their number or their activity, *to juftify the ftake of this province, for the uncertain advantages that might attend immediate junction with them.* There is reafon to believe that fuch muft have been the rifk.

Whilft this army lay at Charlotteburgh, George-Town was taken from the militia by the rebels ; and the whole country to the eaft of the Santée, gave fuch proofs of general defection, that even the militia of the High Hills could not be prevailed upon to join a party of troops who were fent to protect our boats upon the river. The defeat of Major Ferguson, had fo difpirited this part of the country, and

indeed

indeed the loyal subjects were so wearied by the long continuance of the campaign, that Lieutenant-colonel Cruger, (commanding at Ninety-six) sent information to Earl Cornwallis, that the whole district had determined to submit as soon as the rebels should enter it. From these circumstances, from the consideration that delay does not extinguish our hopes in North Carolina; and from the long fatigue of the troops, which made it seriously requisite to give some refreshment to the army; Earl Cornwallis has resolved to remain for the present in a position which may secure the frontiers without separating his force. In this situation we shall be always ready for movement, whensoever opportunity shall recommend it, or circumstances require it. But the first care must be to put Camden and Ninety-six into a better state of defence, and to furnish them with ample stores and salt provisions. Earl Cornwallis foresees all the difficulties of a defensive war. *Yet his Lordship thinks they cannot be weighed against the dangers which must have attended an obstinate adherence to his former plan.* I am instructed by Earl Cornwallis to express, in the strongest terms, his Lordship's feelings, with regard to the very effectual measures which your Excellency had taken to forward his operations. His Lordship hopes that his fears of abusing your Excellency's goodness in that particular, may not have led him to neglect making use of a force intended by your Excellency

Ecellency to be employed by him. But as his Lordſhip knew not how far your Excellency might aim at other objects in the Cheſapeak (to which point his Lordſhip's entreaty for co-operation was originally confined) he could not think of aſſuming the power to order Major-general Leſlie to Cape Fear river; though he pointed out the utility of the meaſure, in caſe it ſhould be conceived within the extent of your Excellency's purpoſe.

Lord Cornwallis farther deſires me to ſay he feels infinitely obliged by the very flattering teſtimonies of approbation with which your Excellency has been pleaſed to honour his ſucceſs on the 16th of Auguſt. He has ſignified your Excellency's thanks to the officers and men, who received them with grateful acknowledgement.

I have the honour to be, &c.

(Signed) RAWDON.

Extract. — *From* **Lord Rawdon** *to Sir Henry Clinton, dated Camp between Broad River, and the Catawba, South Carolina, October* 31, 1780.

SIR,

BY Lord Cornwallis's directions, I had the honour of writing to your Excellency on the 29th Inſtant,

Inftant, detailing to your Excellency the circumftances which had obliged Lord Cornwallis to relinquifh the attempt of penetrating to Hillfborough; and inclofing the copy of a letter which his Lordfhip made me write to Major-general Leflie on that occafion.

On farther confideration his Lordfhip reflecting on the difficulties of a defenfive war, and of the hopes which your Excellency would probably build of our fuccefs in this quarter, has thought it advifable not only to recommend more ftrongly to Major-general Leflie, a plan which may enable us to take an active part; but even to make it his requeft in cafe it fhould not be incompatible with your Excellency's farther arrangements.

Lord Cornwallis is particularly induced to invite Major-general Leflie to co-operation in the Cape Fear river, by the fuppofition that your Excellency may not want thefe troops during the winter: *and they may join your Excellency in the fpring, fcarcely later than, fhould they on the approach of that feafon fail from any part of Chefapeak Bay.*

Extract. — *From Earl Cornwallis to Major-general Leslie, dated Camp at Winnesborough, between Broad River and Wateree, November* 12, 1780.

IF you come to Cape Fear, of which at present, I have little doubt, by the help of gallies and small craft, which will be sent from Charles-town, you will easily secure a water conveyance for your stores up to Cross Creek. I will on hearing of your arrival in Cape Fear river, instantly march with every thing that can be safely spared from this Province, which I am sorry to say is most exceedingly disaffected, to join you at Cross Creek. We will then give our friends in North Carolina, a fair trial. If they behave like men it may be of the greatest advantage to the affairs of Britain. If they are as ——————— as our friends to the southward, we must leave them to their fate, *and secure what we have got.*

Extract. — *From Lieutenant-colonel Balfour, without date, to Major-general Leslie.*

My Dear General,

I WROTE you a few days ago by the Express sloop, and have only to repeat, that the *safety* of this province *now* is concerned in your getting as fast as possible near us. ———— Gates is advancing as we are told, to this province, and already near it.

Copy.— From Sir Henry Clinton, K. B. to Earl Cornwallis, dated New York, December 13, 1780.

MY LORD,

I AM honoured with your Lordship's letters of the 3d and 22d of September, by the Thames, which arrived here the 12th ultimo. And on the 5th instant I received by the Beaumont, those from Lord Rawdon, and Colonel Balfour, to General Leslie. Inclosed I send your Lordship a return of the force that embarked with him.

It was all I could spare; and I thought it fully adequate to the services required. My first instructions to General Leslie put that corps entirely subject to your Lordship's orders.

I did not, I confess, however suppose it would move to Cape Fear; but having afterwards too good reason to dread Ferguson's fate, I in a second instruction recommended that measure, as the only salutary one under the circumstances I apprehended Ferguson's defeat would place your Lordship. By a letter of Colonel Balfour's to General Leslie (without date) are these Expressions " I have only to repeat that the *safety* of this province *now* is concerned in your

getting

getting as fast as possible near us." I should be sorry to understand by this that the province is really in danger. Wishing however to give your Lordship's operations in North Carolina, every assistance in my power, though I can ill spare it, I have sent another expedition into the Chesapeak, under the orders of Brigadier-general Arnold, Lieutenant-colonels Dundas, and Simcoe. The force by land is not equal to that which sailed with General Leslie; but I am not without hopes it will operate most essentially in favour of your Lordship; either by striking at Gates's depot at Petersburg, which I have still reason to think is considerable; or finally by taking post at Portsmouth, which I have ever considered as very important, for reasons most obvious. If we take post there, fortify, and assemble the inhabitants; it ought not afterwards to be quitted, and therefore I cannot suppose your Lordship will wish to alter the disposition of this corps, without absolute necessity.

On the contrary I flatter myself, that should your success be such as your Lordship will, I hope, *now* have reason to expect, that you will reinforce that corps, and enable it to act offensively. When that is your intention, I am to request that the following corps may in their turn be considered for that service, *viz*. The troop of seventeenth dragoons, the yagers, the detachment of the seventeenth foot, and the provincial light infantry, &c. I need not tell your Lordship that these detachments have left me very bare indeed of troops; nor that Washington still continues very strong (at least 12000 men) that he has not detatched a single man as yet to the southward, except Lee's cavalry (about two hundred and fifty). I need not tell you also that there are six thousand French already at Rhode Island — but I must acquaint your Lordship that six complete regiments more are expected, under convoy of a number of capital ships. But whatever may have been the intention of the French in sending a reinforcement to this country, I think the season is now too far advanced to expect the last; and was I not clearly of that opinion I should scarcely dare detatch as I do. As I have always said, I think your Lordship's movement to the southward most important, and as I ever have done, so I will now give them all the assistance I can. It remains to be proved whether we have friends in North Carolina — I am sure we had three years ago — That experiment now will *be fairly tried*; if it succeeds, and we hold the entrance of the Chesapeak — I think the rebels will scarcely risk another attempt upon those provinces.

Copy.

Copy. — *From Earl Cornwallis to Sir Henry Clinton, dated Camp at Wynnesborough, December* 3, 1780.

SIR,

I AM honoured with your letters of the 5th and 6th of last month. Lord Rawdon, during my illness, informed your Excellency, in his letters of the 28th and 31st of October, of the various causes which prevented my penetrating into North Carolina. I shall not trouble you with a recapitulation, except a few words about poor Major Ferguson. I had the honour to inform your Excellency that Major Ferguson had taken infinite pains with some of the militia of Ninety-six. He obtained my permission to make an incursion into Tryon county, while the sickness of my army prevented my moving. As he had only militia and the small remains of his own corps, without baggage or artillery, and as he promised to come back if he heard of any superior force, I thought he could do no harm, and might help to keep alive the spirit of our friends in North Carolina, which might be damped by the slowness of our motions. The event proved unfortunate, without any fault of Major Ferguson's. A numerous and unexpected enemy came from the mountains. As they had good horses,

their

their movements were rapid. Major Ferguson was tempted to stay near the mountains longer than he intended, in hopes of cutting off Colonel Clarke on his return from Georgia. He was not aware that the enemy was so near him; and, in endeavouring to execute my orders of passing the Catawba, and joining me at Charlotte-town, he was attacked by a very superior force, and totally defeated on King's-mountain.

Wynnesborough, my present position, is an healthy spot, well situated to protect the greatest part of the Northern frontier, and to assist Camden and Ninety-six. The militia of the latter, on which alone we could place the smallest dependence, was so totally dispirited by the defeat of Ferguson, that of the whole district we could with difficulty assemble one hundred; and even those, I am convinced, would not have made the smallest resistance if they had been attacked. I determined to remain at this place until an answer arrived from General Leslie, on which my plan for the winter was to depend; and to use every possible means of putting the province into a state of defence, which I found to be absolutely necessary, whether my campaign was offensive or defensive. Bad as the state of our affairs was on the Northern frontier, the Eastern part was much worse. Colonel Tynes, who commanded the militia of the high hills of Santee, and who was posted on Black-river, was surprized and taken, and his men lost all their arms. Colonel Marion had so wrought on the minds of the people, partly by the terror of his threats and cruelty of his punishments; and partly by the promise of plunder, that there was scarcely an inhabitant between the Santée and Pedée, that was not in arms against us. Some parties had even crossed the Santée, and carried terror to the gates of Charles-town. My first object was to reinstate matters in that quarter, without which Camden could receive no supplies. I therefore sent Tarleton, who pursued Marion for several days, obliged his corps to take to the swamps, and by convincing the inhabitants that there was a power superior to Marion, who could likewise reward and punish, so far checked the insurrection, that the greatest part of them have not dared to appear in arms against us since his expedition. ———

——— As it will be necessary to drive back the enemies army, and at the same time to maintain a superiority on both our flanks; and as I thought the co-operation of General Leslie, even at the distance of Cape-Fear river, would be attended with many difficulties, I have sent cruizers off the Frying-pan to bring him into Charles-town, and I hourly expect his arrival.

After every thing that has happened, I will not presume to make your Excellency any san-

guine

guine promises. *The force you have sent me is greater than I expected; and full as much as I think you could possibly spare*, unless the enemy detached in force to the Southward. The utmost exertion of my abilities shall be used to employ them to the best advantage.

Whenever our operations commence, your Excellency may depend on hearing from me as frequently as possible; and it is from events alone that any future plan can be proposed.

Extract. ----- From Earl Cornwallis to Sir Henry Clinton, dated Wynnesborough, Dec. 22, 1780.

SIR,

I HAVE the honour to inform your Excellency, that Major-general Leslie arrived with his whole fleet at Charles-town on the 14th of this month, with no other loss than the dragoon horses, and a great part of those for the Quarter-master-general. The species of troops which compose the reinforcement are, exclusive of the Guards and regiment of Bose, exceedingly bad.[*] I do not mean,
by

[*] When his Lordship made this remark, he had not seen the troops. He must have, therefore, formed his opinion from the report of others. But in justice to the corps who are spoken so slightingly of, it is necessary

Second Move into North Carolina. 49

by representing this to your Excellency, to insinuate, that you have not sent every assistance to me which you could with prudence and safety spare from New-York. From the account which your Excellency does me the honour to send me, of the situation and strength of General Washington's army, and the French force at Rhode-Island, I am convinced that you have done so. But I think it but justice to the troops serving in this district to state the fact, lest the services performed by the Southern army should appear inadequate to what might be expected from the numbers of which it may appear to consist. The fleet from New-York, with the recruits, arrived a few days before General Leslie. ⸺⸺⸺

cessary to observe, that they have all behaved in such a manner as to merit the applauses of the officers commanding them, and one of them (Fannings) has obtained a British establishment.

PART V.

CONTAINING

EXTRACTS

FROM THE

Correspondence; between his Lordship's second Move into North Carolina, and his Arrival at Wilmington.

Extract. — *From Earl Cornwallis to Sir Henry Clinton, dated Wynnesborough, Jan.* 6, 1781.

SIR,

I AM just honoured with your letter of the 13th ult. I have written several letters in the course of last month, to give your Excellency an account of the state of the provinces of South Carolina and Georgia, and of the military transactions. I fear they are all still at Charles-town, as no opportunity has offered of transmitting them to New-York. The present addition to the naval force

force in this quarter, will, I hope, enable me; or, if I am too diftant, Lieutenant-colonel Balfour, to tranfmit reports more frequently.

The difficulties I have had to ftruggle with, have not been occafioned by the oppofite army. They always keep at a confiderable diftance, and difappear on our approach.

But the conftant incurfions of Refugees, North Carolinians, and Back-Mountain-men, and the perpetual rifings in the different parts of this province; the invariable fucceffes of all thefe parties againft our militia, keep the whole country in continual alarm, and renders the affiftance of regular troops every where neceffary. Your Excellency will judge of this by the difpofition of the troops, which I have the honour to enclofe to you.

I fhall begin my march to-morrow, (having been delayed a few days by a diverfion made by the enemy towards Ninety-fix) and propofe keeping on the Weft of Catawba for a confiderable diftance. I fhall then proceed to pafs that river, and the Yadkin. Events alone can decide the future fteps. I fhall take every opportunity of communicating with Brigadier-general Arnold.

Extract. — *From Major-general Leslie to Sir Henry Clinton, dated Camden, Jan. 8, 1781.*

SIR,

I ARRIVED here some days ago, with the Guards, the regiment of Bose, and Yagers; I went to Wynnesborough to see Earl Cornwallis. He moves to-day, and I march to-morrow with the above troops and North-Carolina regiment. I meet his Lordship about seventy miles from hence.

The troops are exceeding healthy, and the weather has been very favourable.

Copy. — *From Sir Henry Clinton to Earl Cornwallis, dated New-York, March 2, 5, and 8, 1781.*

[Sent by Captain Amherst, in the Jupiter Merchant Ship.]

March 2d.

MY LORD,

YOUR Lordship may probably hear, that the army and navy in the Chesapeak are blocked up by a superior French naval force to that under Captain Symonds. The first account I had of it was

Relative to the Move to Wilmington.

was from General Arnold, dated February 14, and I sent it immediately to the Admiral at Gardiner's-bay. A day or two afterwards I had it confirmed, that they were part of the fleet from Rhode-island, which I have heard since sailed from thence on the 9th ult. Notwithstanding which I greatly fear he has not sent a naval force to relieve them. Washington has detached some New-England troops under La Fayette and Howe that way.

March 5th.

IF so much time is given, I cannot answer for consequences. Portsmouth is safe at this season against any attack from the Suffolk side, but not so from a landing in any of the bays to the Southward of Elizabeth-river.

I have much to lament that the Admiral did not think it advisable to send there at first, as Brigadier-general Arnold's move in favour of your Lordship's operations will have been stopped. — And if the Admiral delays it too long, I shall dread still more fatal consequences.

I have troops already embarked in a great proportion to that of the enemy, but to send them under two frigates only, before the Chesapeak is our own, is to sacrifice the troops and their convoy.

I enclose

I enclose your Lordship all the news I have been able to collect. —— —— has, I think, quitted Congress, and put them at defiance. — Your Lordship will see his plan by the newspaper of the 28th of February, said to be genuine. Discontent runs high in Connecticut. In short, my Lord, there seems little wanting to give a mortal stab to rebellion but a proper reinforcement and a superiority at sea for the next campaign; without which, any enterprize depending on water movements must certainly run great risk. Should the troops already embarked for the Chesapeak proceed, and, when there, be able to undertake any operation in addition to what Brigadier-general Arnold proposes, I am confident it will be done. Major-general Phillips will command this expedition.

Till Colonel Bruce arrives, I am uncertain what reinforcements are intended for this army. The minister has, however, assured me, that every possible exertion will be made.

I shall tremble for our post at Portsmouth, should the enemy's reinforcement arrive in that neighbourhood before the force, which I *now* flatter myself the Admiral will order a sufficient convoy for, arrives.

March

March 8th.

I HAVE received a letter from General Arnold, dated the 25th ult. wherein he tells me, that the French left him on the 19th.

And in another letter, of the 27th, he says, he has not the least doubt of defending his post against the force of the country and two thousand French troops, until a reinforcement can arrive from New-York. And that he proposed to send five hundred men, under Colonel Dundas, up James-river, to make a diversion in favour of your Lordship.

The Admiral informs me of the return of the French ships to Rhode-island, and of their having taken the Romulus, and carried her into that place. But as the Admiral, in his letter of the 4th, seems to think, that the whole, or at least a great part of the French fleet sailed for the Chesapeak on the 27th ult, and that he was at that time ready to sail, I flatter myself he is either gone there, or has sent a sufficient force to clear the Chesapeak. The troops under General Phillips have been embarked for some time, and are now at the Hook waiting for the Admiral, or a message from him. General Phillips commands, and I am sure you know his inclinations are to
co-operate

co-operate with your Lordship; and you will therefore be pleased to take him under your orders, until you hear farther from me.

I have the honour, &c.

(Signed) H. CLINTON.

Extract. — *From Brigadier-general Arnold to Sir Henry Clinton, K. B. dated Portsmouth, January* 23, 1781.

THE line of works begun, which are necessary for the defence of this place, your Excellency will observe (by the plan inclosed) are very extensive, and from the situation of it, cannot be contracted. The engineer's opinion of them, and the number of men necessary for their defence, against a superior force, I do myself the honour to inclose. Lieutenant-colonels Dundas and Simcoe, are clearly of opinion with me, that three thousand men are necessary for their defence. We have all been greatly deceived in the extent and nature of the ground. There are many places in the river much easier defended with half the number of men. From the sketch of the place your Excellency will judge whether our opinion is well founded or not.

This province and North Carolina, are collecting the militia, undoubtedly with a view to pay us a visit. Their numbers, from the best information I can obtain, are four thousand or five thousand. At present I can hardly imagine they will attack this post, though the works are of no manner of service to us; and all our force cannot complete them in three months: I therefore think it my duty to request a reinforcement of at least two thousand men, which would render the post permanent and secure against any force the country could bring, as detachments could always be made (leaving the garrison secure) to disperse the militia, whenever it was found they were collecting; and the advantages of transportation, which we may derive from light boats (of which I propose to build fifty) would enable us to move with double the celerity, that the militia could do with every exertion.

The country people have not come in, in numbers, as I expected; the necessity of General Leslie's removing from this place, after their being assured of his intention to remain here, has impressed them with the idea that we shall do the same; which is not easily effaced, as they have many of them suffered severely since his departure. I have not with certainty been informed where he is at present — Reports, which are contradictory, say at Cape Fear; others that he is at Charles-town, and some say at neither. I know not what opinion to form; neither have I heard from Lord Cornwallis, but by reports, which say he is at or near Camden — No opportunity has yet presented of writing to either of these gentlemen — but I am of opinion our diversion at Richmond will operate much in his favour, as I am informed the militia and light-horse, sent to reinforce the rebel army, under Greene, have been ordered to return.

Extract.

Extract. — *From Sir Henry Clinton, K. B. to General Earl Cornwallis, dated New York, February 5, 1781.*

MY LORD,

I HAVE the honour to inclose to your Lordship the copy of a letter I have lately received from Brigadier-general Arnold, by which you will perceive that with scarcely one thousand men (for several of his transports, that had been separated on the voyage, had not then rejoined him) he penetrated to Richmond, the capital of Virginia, and has rendered important service, by destroying a valuable foundry, a considerable quantity of public stores, cannon, &c. &c. Indeed the whole of his operations upon the occasion appear to have been conducted in a manner which strongly marks his character of a very active and good officer — and I sincerely hope, that this important stroke will essentially aid your Lordship's operations.

Extract. — *From Sir H. Clinton, K. B. to Lieutenant-colonel Balfour, sent by Captain Amherst, in the Jupiter merchant ship, dated New York, March 9, 1781.*

SIR,

I WAS favoured with your letters, dated the 25th and 31st January, and 2d and 5th February, by the Halifax sloop of war, on the 16th ultimo.

Captain Amherst of the sixtieth regiment, who is so obliging to charge himself with my dispatches for Lord Cornwallis, will deliver them to your care.

Extract. — *From Brigadier-general Arnold to Sir H. Clinton, K. B. dated Portsmouth, February 13, 1781.*

NO time has been lost in repairing the old, and erecting new works here, in which the negroes have been very serviceable, but none are yet complete. Repairing barracks, foraging, and patrolling with large parties, have engrossed the time of a great part of the troops. One hundred men are posted at the great bridge.

Lieutenant-colonel Simcoe, with near four hundred men, are in Princess Anne county; scouring the county of several parties, and arranging matters with the country people.

The

The enemy are at Suffolk, with two thoufand five hundred, or three thoufand men; they threaten an attack upon us, but I cannot fuppofe them capable of fo much temerity. We are prepared for them at all points, and I believe nothing will induce them to attack us, but the hope of fucceeding in a furprife, and defpair of keeping their tattered force together, through want of provifions, and the neceffity of their ploughing their lands, to prevent a famine the enfuing year.

Extract. — *From Brigadier general Arnold to Sir H. Clinton, K. B. dated Portfmouth, February* 25, 1781.

AFTER my difpatches were clofed (which were intended to go by the General Monk) three French fhips, one a fixty-four, the other two frigates, arrived from Rhode Ifland, and anchored in Lynhaven Bay. On the 14th inftant they arrived in Hampton road, and remained there until the 19th, when they left the Capes, and are faid to be now cruizing to the fouthward of them.

Before the arrival of the French fhips, the enemy's force did not exceed two thoufand five hundred men, at Suffolk and in the vicinity, which was greatly augmented

augmented soon after their arrival. On the 18th they came down in force, near our lines, and surprised a piquet of six men; but soon retired. Lieutenant-colonel Simcoe with four hundred men being in Princess Anne county, I did not think it prudent to leave our works to attack them.

I have very good intelligence that the rebels at Suffolk have been informed by express from General Greene, that on the 16th or 18th instant, my Lord Cornwallis crossed the Dan river, sixty miles above Halifax, and one hundred and twelve from Petersburgh, with one thousand cavalry and four thousand infantry, and was on the march for Petersburgh. Generals Greene and Morgan, with three thousand or four thousand men, chiefly militia, were retiring before him; in consequence of which a considerable part of their troops, have been detached to join General Greene. I have not been able to ascertain the number of troops remaining at Suffolk and in the vicinity; I expect to do it in a day or two, in which time every possible effort shall be made to complete our works in such a manner, that a considerable detachment may be made to proceed up the James river, with some ships to co-operate with Lord Cornwallis; and if he should have reached the river, to furnish him with such supplies of provisions, &c. as we can spare, and his troops be most in need of.

Extract.

Extract. — From Sir *Henry Clinton*, K. B. to Brigadier-general *Arnold*, dated *New York*, *February* 18, 1781.

APPEARANCES at Rhode Island give me reason to suppose that the ships seen last Wednesday were the avant garde from that place. Should they pay you a visit from Rhode Island, you may rest assured every attention will be paid to our situation, and that our movements will be regulated by theirs.

I am afraid Tarleton's affair is too true; but I have reason notwithstanding to believe Lord Cornwallis is far advanced in Carolina.

Extract. — From Brigadier-general *Arnold* to Sir H. *Clinton*, K. B. dated *Portsmouth*, *February* 27, 1781.

I HAVE not the least doubt that every possible attention will be paid to our situation. We are under no apprehensions at present from the force of the country; and if the French should detach from Rhode Island to this place, I have not the least doubt of defending it against the force of the country and two thousand French troops, until a reinforcement can arrive from New York.

To-

To-morrow I intend embarking some stores, and the next day about five hundred troops under the orders of Lieutenant-colonel Dundas, to proceed up the James river, to make a diversion in favour of my Lord Cornwallis.

Copy. — *Sir Henry Clinton, K. B. to Brigadier-general Arnold, dated New York, March* 1, 1781.

SIR,

I SUPPOSE of course that the admiral, who knew your situation on the 21st, and heard at the same time, that the sixty-four and two frigates were from Rhode Island, has detached to your relief; — lest he should not, I have repeatedly pressed him to do it since.

The French fleet has not yet sailed from Rhode Island; if it does, encumbered with troops, the admiral will of course follow without incumbrance; and, when he has fixed them, it will be time enough to send troops. In case a fleet should appear under French colours, do not be alarmed, as I shall advise the admiral to send in that manner, to deceive the enemy.

There is information of from twelve to fourteen hundred troops being at Brunswick the 27th of February, on their way to the southward. These it is our business to watch.

The troops which are all ready embarked, are detained till I receive certain advice that the French ships are removed from the Chesapeak, there being nothing here but frigates to convoy them.

I have received a letter this day from the admiral, dated the 4th: he has given me no pofsitive information of the movements of the French; he will send a ship to observe their situation in Rhode Island, and will proceed accordingly. Should he call here, the troops will in all probability sail with him; if he does not, I shall send them as soon as I know the way to the Chesapeak is clear.

Extract.— From Instructions to Major-general Phillips, dated New York, March 10, 1781.

SIR,

YOU will be pleased to proceed with the troops embarked under your command, to Chesapeak Bay; and there form a junction as soon as possible with brigadier-general Arnold, whom, and the corps with him, you will take under your orders.

When you shall have formed your junction with Brigadier general Arnold, if you find that General acting under the orders of Earl Cornwallis, you will of course endeavour to fulfil those orders. If this should

should not be the case; after receiving every information respecting his probable situation, you will make such movements with the corps (*then* under your orders), as can be made consistent with the security of the post on Elizabeth river, or you shall think will most effectually assist his Lordship's operations; by destroying or taking any magazines, the enemy may have on James river, or at Petersburg, on the Appamatox.

The object of co-operation with Lord Cornwallis, being fulfilled, you are at liberty to carry on such desultory expeditions for the purpose of destroying the enemy's public stores and magazines in any part of the Chesapeak as you shall judge proper.

If the admiral's disapproving of Portsmouth, and requiring a fortified station for large ships in the Chesapeak, should propose *York Town,* or *Old Point Comfort,* if possession of either can be acquired and maintained *without great risk, or loss,* you are at liberty to take possession thereof. *But if the objections are such as you think forcible, you must, after stating those objections, decline it, till solid operation take place in the Chesapeak.*

Concerning your return to this place, you will receive either my orders, or Lord Cornwallis's, as circumstances may make necessary.

It is probable that when the objects of this expedition are fulfilled, and you have strengthened the present works, and added such others as you shall think necessary,

neceſſary, you *may return to this place*. In which caſe you muſt bring with you, Brigadier-general Arnold, the light infantry, Colonel Robinſon's corps, or the ſeventy-ſixth; and if it ſhould be poſſible, the Queen's rangers. The moment you have communicated with Lord Cornwallis, and heard from his Lordſhip, you are to conſider yourſelf as under his Lordſhip's orders, until he, or you ſhall hear further from me.

(Signed) H. CLINTON.

Extract. — *From Brigadier-general Arnold to Sir Henry Clinton, dated Portſmouth, March* 8, 1781.

ON the 6th I received information that Lord Cornwallis had not penetrated further than the Dan or Roanoke river, and that, in conſequence of the miſinformation (ſent to the rebel army, by expreſs, as mentioned in my laſt) being contradicted, their detachment had returned to their army at Suffolk, as well as Mr. Gregory, to the north-weſt bridge — Their force at the former place three thouſand, at the latter five hundred. On this change of affairs the troops under the orders of Lieutenant-colonel Dundas, who were deſigned up the James river, were countermanded.

The enemy within two days have moved with their force, said to be upwards of three thousand men to Pricket mills, twelve miles from this place, and threaten an attack upon us. I have every rerson to believe they have collected their force to co-operate with the French ships and troops, which they hourly expect from Rhode island.

Extract. — *From Admiral Arbuthnot to General Arnold, dated Chesapeak, March* 19, 1781.

THE French fleet sailed from Rhode-island on or about the 8th instant, intending a co-operation with Mr. Washington, to attack you. I followed them on the 10th, and came up with them on the 16th: an action ensued of about an hour and an half, when they fled off with their whole squadron.

I shall put to sea again immediately with the squadron, and endeavour to bring them to a second action. Should I be unable to do so, I shall return with the squadron to New York, which must be exposed in my absence, and I must withdraw the ships that are now with you.

Extract.

Extract. — *From Major-general Phillips to Sir Henry Clinton, dated Chesapeak, on board the Royal Oak, in Lynhaven Bay, March 26, 1781.*

'THE fleet containing the troops under my orders, arrived off the Chesapeak yesterday, when Captain Hudson gave the Orpheus liberty to make sail and carry me into this bay, where we knew by intelligence from frigates we met at sea, that Admiral Arbuthnot was with his fleet.

Our fleet sailed from the Hook on Tuesday the 20th instant, and with variable winds, and good weather, is arrived; and now beating up to the rendezvous at Hampton, with hopes, not a certainty, of getting there this evening.

With respect to intelligence, it is not in my power to give you any at a certainty. I hear that at York the rebels have been and are fortifying, and that there are heavy cannon there.

Extract. — *From Sir Henry Clinton to Major-general Phillips, dated New York, March 24, 1781.*

I BELIEVE that Lord Cornwallis has finished his campaign, and if report says true, very handsomely, by taking all Greene's cannon, and recovering the

the greatest part of his own men who had been made prisoners by Mr. Greene. If that should be the case, and Lord Cornwallis should not want any co-operation to assist him, and you see no prospect of striking an important stroke elsewhere, I shall probably request you and General Arnold to return to me with such troops as I have already named in my instructions. But all this will depend on the information I shall receive from you, and your opinion, respecting the post of Portsmouth, and such others as you propose to establish on James river, with their importance, considered, either as assisting Lord Cornwallis's operations, or connected with those of the navy.

You will probably hear from Lord Cornwallis before you determine on any attempt at a distance from him. I wish much to know what force he can spare from the troops under his Lordship's immediate orders; for till I do, it is impossible to fix any plan. Three complete regiments will, I hope, arrive at Charles-town, in the course of a few days, if Captain Elphinston should think it too early in the season to come directly here; and three more are hourly expected from the West Indies; both which divisions will of course join me.

The French certainly expect an early reinforcement. If it comes from Europe, we must, I think, hear from thence long before it arrives; if from the' Havannah, copper-bottomed sloops or frigates, which the admiral will doubtlefs have on the look-out, will announce their arrival, and give you time to determine, what in that cafe, is beft to be done.

And here, I take the liberty of hinting to you, that (from the appearance on the map when you have once obtained a naval force in Curratuck and Albemarle founds, by holding the bridges of Pequimans and Pafquotank rivers, you fecure a fhort paffage acrofs the Albemarle found, and communication with Lord Cornwallis; or, by deftroying the bridges on thofe rivers, you prevent the enemy's approach by the bridge at Northweft-landing.

Extract. — *Major General Phillips to Sir Henry Clinton, K. B. dated Portfmouth, April* 3, 1781.

I have from the moment of my landing here, purfued the firft object of your Excellency's inftructions: "The fecurity of the poft upon Elizabeth "river, near the mouth of James river."

And your Excellency may be affured, I fhall ufe every means to attain this very material purpofe, fo neceffary, and which alone can enable me, with four thoufand militia in our front and near us, to purfue the fecond part of your inftructions: "A move in force

force upon the enemy's communications between Virginia and North Carolina, at Petersburgh, in assistance to Lord Cornwallis." And I shall do this the moment it may be possible, consistent with the security of the post on Elizabeth river.

It is unlucky for us, that we know so little of Lord Cornwallis, in favour of whom, and his operations we are directed by your Excellency to exert our utmost attention. I shall do all in my power to assist and co-operate with his Lordship, and shall from inclination, as well as in obedience to your Excellency's instructions, do all I can to effect this most desirable end.

I apprehend from various rebel accounts that Lord Cornwallis, although he kept the field, has suffered very much after the action of the 15th ultimo, and to be fortifying to the west of the *Haw* river, near Guildford, which seems a good position, having that river in front of the communication quite down to Cross-Creek and Cape Fear.

Should his Lordship want support, he must in course draw it from Charles-town to Cape Fear river, by directing Lord Rawdon to abandon the frontier, and keep only a garrison in Charles-town.

I embrace your idea, Sir, that should La Fayette remain at Annapolis, which must proceed from the enemy's fear of being attacked in Maryland, it will be possible to carry him Annapolis and Baltimore; and if you will send me the British grenadiers and

forty-

forty-second regiment, I will, with almost certain hopes of success, go upon the attempt; and will make an expedition in Virginia at the same instant, as shall effectually prevent any support from thence to Maryland.

I come now to the particulars of this post, and as it is not possible in so short a time, to go through the proper form of a regular report of the commanding engineer, who came with me, I will, until that can be done, very freely offer my opinion that it has not been, I should imagine, properly explained to your Excellency, by Generals Matthews and Leslie. The object of the post, from its situation, respecting James river and the Chesapeak, with its connection with the waters to and in Albemarle sound, and the consequent connections it may have with any army in the Carolinas, are subjects I do not think myself at liberty to touch upon. I mean to confine myself merely to the locality of the post itself; and under that description, I declare, I think the present situation not calculated for a post of force, or for one for a small number of troops. In the first idea, I think three points should be taken, as at *Mill Point* and *Norfolk* positively; the third must depend on more examination of the Elizabeth river, than I have yet been able to give. These points taken would mutually assist the navy stationed here, which might lay within, and be protected; and one point forced, a retreat is left by the other two: and your Excellency will immediately observe, that it must require a large force indeed, to attack the three points at once.

Should it be required by your Excellency merely to keep a post here, without intending more than a station, I think Mill Point, where the old fort stood, well calculated for such a purpose; and it would require not more than a strong battalion equal to six hundred effective rank and file to be the garrison.

In both instances the Chesapeak must be secure, for even allowing every exertion of defence against a fleet, it would be difficult to preserve the river under the first idea of an extensive plan. Under the latter, I consider it scarcely to be done. Old Point Comfort shall be explored, as it seems a point which a small force might defend, and the shipping have scope to act in, and by trying various methods of winds and tides, would be able possibly to escape from even a superior naval force; whereas, once blocked up in Elizabeth river, the ships must at last fall with the post.

I come now to the Norfolk and Princess Ann counties, where we cannot much depend for assistance. They are timorous, cautious, at best, but half friends, and perhaps some, if not many, concealed enemies. Supposing them perfectly ours, we should not be able to arm more than five or six hundred men, who would become a charge to us while we remained, and being left, would be undone: At present, they act a sort of saving game, but are of no use to us. Upon the whole, Sir, it may be perceived that I lean in favour of a small post, where the army can assist the navy, and the latter have a chance of escaping, supposing a superior force to arrive in the bay; and where the post can be maintained with five or six hundred men, for some time, even perhaps till some reinforcement *naval* and land might be sent to raise a siege.

Copy. — *Sir Henry Clinton, K. B. to Major-general Phillips, dated New-York, April 5, 1781.*

DEAR SIR,

I NEED not say how important success in the Highlands would be. I beg you will without loss of time, consult General Arnold upon the subject. I beg I may have his project, and your opinion, as well as his, respecting it, as soon as possible. When I have considered it, and if I determine to undertake it, I will send for him; and if operation should be at a stand in the Chesapeak at the time, I will request you also to be of the party; the proportion of artillery I desired you to make, will of course be ready.

P. S.

P. S. If General Arnold does not think it expedient at *this time* to attempt it, which however, I should be sorry for, perhaps a combined move between us against Philadelphia, may take place. You, by landing at the head of Elk; I, at Newcastle, or Chester;—if the first, General Arnold must let me have his plan as soon as possible, and be ready to follow it himself, or may bring it, if you can spare him.

Extract.— *Sir Henry Clinton, K. B. to Major-general Phillips, dated New-York, April* 13, 1781.

In addition to what I have said in those letters (April 5) I scarce need mention, that I am persuaded you will not delay to make such movements in favour of Lord Cornwallis as you judge best, with the force you have left after garrisoning the different works at Portsmouth; which after reading the report of your engineer, I flatter myself will be perfectly secure with six or eight hundred men. In that case you will be at liberty to act with the remainder, being as good troops as any in this country, in such operations as you shall judge most conducive to assist those of his Lordship.

Extract

Extract.—Major-general Phillips to Sir Henry Clinton, dated Portsmouth, in Virginia, April 15, 1781.

I AM free to declare Portsmouth to be a bad post, its locality not calculated for defence, the collateral points necessary to be taken up so many, that altogether it would require so great a number of troops as no general officer I imagine would venture to propose to the Commander-in-chief to leave here for mere defence —— A spot might be found, I apprehend, for a post for five hundred men, should it be necessary to have one in Elizabeth River.

Extract.—Major-general Phillips to Sir Henry Clinton, dated Hampton Road, on board the Maria, April 19, 1781.

THE face of affairs seems changed, and the Carolinas, like all America, are lost in rebellion. My letters of the 15th, 16th, and yesterday, will go now in the Amphitrite, for I stopped the express boat last night.—I have nothing farther to add, than that I conceive Lord Cornwallis will not have it in his power to bring with him many troops, it will depend on your Excellency from his Lordship's

letters,

letters, and from those of Brigdier-general Arnold and me, whether you shall think it proper to have an operation in force in Chesapeak — if yes, the troops here are too few — if no, too many.

I hope to hear from your Excellency directly, and perhaps it may not be so well to trust such a serious dispatch, as your next, Sir, will probably be, to an unarmed vessel, but that a frigate will be sent.

The operations I had proposed against Williamsburg, shall take place to-morrow morning, but I think it my duty to call a council of war, circumstanced as Lord Cornwallis is, to judge whether an attempt on Petersburg may now be proper.

Extract. — *Lieutenant-colonel Balfour to Sir Henry Clinton, received by the Amphitrite man of war, dated Charles-Town, April 7, 1781.*

SIR,

I AM honoured with your letters of the 2d of January, and 19th of last month; as also with one of the 14th ult. by your Excellency's directions, from Captain Smith.

As Lord Cornwallis is in the greatest want of every supply, I have sent him to Cape Fear what could be procured here, and as he will have many calls

calls on the Hospital, in consequence of the late marches and action, I have taken care to furnish a supply of officers and stores to that department at Wilmington; and shall by that way forward to his Lordship *your Excellency's dispatches*, whenever an occasion offers.

PART VI.

PART VI.

CONTAINING

EXTRACTS

FROM THE

Correspondence; between Lord Cornwallis's arrival at Wilmington, and his entering Virginia.

Extract.— From Earl Cornwallis to Sir Henry Clinton, received by his Majesty's ship Amphitrite, dated Camp, near Wilmington, April 10, 1781.

SIR,

I AM just informed that I have a chance of sending a few lines to New-York by the Amphitrite But as it depends upon my being expeditious, I cannot attempt to give your Excellency a particular account of the winter's campaign, or the battle of Guildford.

I am

I am very anxious to receive your Excellency's commands, being as yet totally in the dark as to the intended operations of the summer. I cannot help expressing my wishes that the Chesapeak may become the seat of war, even (if necessary) at the expence of abandoning New-York. — Until Virginia is in a manner subdued, our hold of the Carolinas must be difficult, if not precarious. The rivers in Virginia are advantageous to an invading army; but North Carolina is, of all the provinces of America, the most difficult to attack (unless material assistance could be got from the inhabitants, the contrary of which I have sufficiently experienced) on account of its great extent, of the numberless rivers and creeks, and the total want of interior navigation.

Copy. — *Sir Henry Clinton to Earl Cornwallis, dated New-York, April* 30, 1781.

MY LORD,

CAPTAIN Biggs of his Majesty's ship Amphitrite, who arrived here the 22d, has delivered to me your Lordship's two letters from Wilmington of the 10th instant, informing me of your having obtained a complete victory over the rebel General Greene, near Guildford, on the 15th ult. On which occasion I beg leave to offer your Lordship my most hearty congratulations, and to request you will present my thanks to Major-general Leslie, Brigadier O'Hara, and Lieutenant-colonel Tarleton, for the great assistance you received from them, and to the officers and men under your command, for their great exertions on the march through Carolina, and their persevering intrepidity in action.

The disparity of numbers between your Lordship's force and that of the enemy opposed to you, appears to be very great; and I confess I am at some loss to guess how your Lordship came to be reduced before the action to one thousand three hundred and sixty infantry,—as by the distribution sent to me in your letter of the 6th of January, I am to suppose it was your intention to take with you the regiments mentioned in the margin,* which (notwithstanding the loss of the seventy-first and legion, in the unfortunate affair of the Cowpens) I should imagine must have amounted to considerably above three thousand, exclusive of cavalry and militia.

Before I was favoured with your Lordship's letter, the rebel account of the battle of Guildford had led me

* Brigade of guards.
Twenty-third.
Seventy-first, two battalions.
Jagers.
Regiment of Bose.
Light infantry seventy-first.
Legion.
North Carolina regiment.

me indeed to hope that its confequences would have been more decifive; and that Green would have repaffed the Roanoke, and left your Lordfhip at liberty to purfue the objects of your move into North Carolina. Under the perfuafion therefore that you would foon be able to finifh your arrangements for the fecurity of the Carolinas, I fubmitted to you in my letter of the 13th inftant (a duplicate of which I have the honour to inclofe) the propriety in that cafe of your going in a frigate to Chefapeak, and directing fuch corps to follow you thither as you judged could be beft fpared. But as it is now probable that your Lordfhip's prefence in Carolina cannot be fo foon difpenfed with, I make no doubt but you will think it right to communicate to Major-general Phillips, without delay, the plan of your future operations in that quarter, together with your opinion how the Chefapeak army can beft direct theirs to affift them. That general officer has already under his orders three thoufand five hundred men, and I fhall fend him one thoufand feven hundred more, which are now embarked, and will fail whenever the Admiral is ready. With thefe, my Lord, which are rank and file fit for duty, and great part of them taken from the elite of my army, General Phillips is directed by his inftructions to act in favour of your Lordfhip to the beft of his own judgment, until he receives your orders; and afterwards in fuch manner as you may please to command him, &c. — But I shall be sorry to find your Lordship continue in the opinion that our hold of the Carolinas must be difficult, if not precarious, until Virginia is in a manner subdued; as that is an event which I fear would require a considerable space of time to accomplish; and as far as I can judge, it might be not quite so expedient at this advanced season of the year to enter into a long operation in that climate. This, however will greatly depend upon circumstances, of which your Lordship and General Phillips may probably be better judges hereafter.

With regard to the operations of the summer, which your Lordship is anxious to receive my directions about, you cannot but be sensible that they must in a great measure depend on your Lordship's successes in Carolina, the certainty and numbers of the expected reinforcement from Europe, and likewise your Lordship's sending back to me the corps I had spared to you under Major-general Leslie (which Lord Rawdon in his letter of the 31st of October told me you could return in the spring) for until I am informed of the particulars of your Lordship's march through North Carolina, the effective strength of your moving army, your plan of operations for carrying those objects you had or may have in view into execution, as well by the corps acting under your immediate orders, as those acting in co-operation under Major-general Phillips, it must be obviously

ously impossible for me to determine finally upon a plan of operations for the campaign.

I was indeed in great hopes that your successes in North Carolina would have been such as to have put it in my power to avail myself of a large portion of your Lordship's army, the whole Chesapeak corps, and the reinforcements from Europe, for this campaign's operations to the northward of Carolina; but I observe with concern from your Lordship's letter, that so far from being in a condition to spare me any part of your present force, you are of opinion that part of the European reinforcement will be indispensibly necessary to enable you to act offensively, or even to maintain yourself in the upper parts of the country.

Had I known what your Lordship's further offensive measures were intended to be for the remaining part of the season, I might now have given an opinion upon them, as well as on the probable co-operation of the corps in Chesapeak; without having which it will be scarcely possible for me to form any. For as I said before, I fear no solid operation can be carried on to the northward of Chesapeak, before those to the southward of it are entirely at an end, either from success or the season; and my letter to your Lordship of the 6th of November will have informed you what were my ideas of the operations proper to be pursued in Chesapeak, and my expectations from them, had circumstances admitted of my

pursuing

pursuing the plan to its full extent. But I must now defer the fixing ultimately on a plan for the campaign, until I am made acquainted with the final success of your Lordship's operations, your prospects and sentiments, and I can judge what force I can collect for such measures as I can then determine upon.

I have the honour, &c.

(Signed) H. CLINTON.

Copy.— From Lieutenant-colonel Balfour to Sir Henry Clinton, received by the Speedy packet, which called at Cape Fear, dated Charles-Town, April 20, 1781.

SIR,

I HAVE the honour to acquaint your Excellency, that by the letters from Lord Rawdon of the 12th, 13th, and 15th instant, there is the fullest information, that General Greene with his army is advancing into this province, and that his light troops have actually passed the Pedee. The object of this movement there is every reason to believe is Camden,

den, which at prefent is but weak, Lord Rawdon having detached Lieutenant-colonel Watfon, with two battalions from that poft; fo that in the end it may be expedient for combining our force, to relinquifh every thing on the other fide Santee — a meafure, however, which your Excellency may be affured will not be taken but in cafe of the utmoft neceffity.

As this movement of Greene's may confiderably change Lord Cornwallis's views, (who is now at Wilmington) I have judged it fit to lay before your Excellency as foon as poffible this intelligence, which is like- wife forwarded to Lord Cornwallis by an exprefs boat.

I have the honour, &c.

(Signed) W. BALFOUR.

Extract of a letter from Lord Rawdon to Lord Corn- wallis, May 24, 1781.

Lieutenant-colonel Balfour was fo good as to meet me at Nelfon's. He took this meafure that he might reprefent his circumftances to me. He ftated that the revolt was univerfal, that from the little reafon to apprehend this ferious invafion,* *the old works of Charles-town had been in part levelled, to make*

* It is prefumable that Colonel Balfour likewife communicated this material information to Lord Cornwallis.

make way for new ones, which were not yet constructed; that its garrison was inadequate to oppose any force of consequence, and that the defection of the town's people shewed itself in a thousand instances. I agreed with him in the conclusion to be drawn from thence, that any misfortune happening to my corps might entail the loss of the province.

Copy.—Earl Cornwallis to Lord George Germain, dated Wilmington, April 23, 1781.

MY LORD,

I YESTERDAY received an express by a small vessel from Charles-Town, informing me that a frigate was there, but not then able to get over the bar, with dispatches from Sir Henry Clinton, notifying to me that Major-general Phillips had been detached into the Chesapeak with a considerable force, with instructions to co-operate with this army, and to put himself under my orders. This express likewise brought me the disagreeable accounts that the upper posts of South Carolina were in the most imminent danger, from an alarming spirit of revolt among many of the people, and by a movement of General Greene's army. Although

Although the expresses which I sent from Cross Creek, to inform Lord Rawdon of the necessity I was under of coming to this place, and to warn him of the possibility of such an attempt of the enemy, had all miscarried; yet his Lordship was lucky enough to be apprized of General Greene's approach, at least six days before he could possibly reach Camden; and I am therefore still induced to hope, from my opinion of his Lordship's abilities and the precautions taken by him and Lieutenant-colonel Balfour, that we shall not be so unfortunate as to lose any considerable corps.

The distance from hence to Camden, the want of forage and subsistence on the greatest part of the road, and the difficulty of passing the Pedee when opposed by an enemy, render it utterly impossible for me to give immediate assistance; and I apprehend a possibility of the utmost hazard to this little corps without the chance of a benefit in the attempt. For, if we are so unlucky as to suffer a severe blow in South Carolina, the spirit of revolt in that province would become very general, and the numerous rebels in this province be encouraged to be more than ever active and violent. This might enable General Greene to hem me in among the Great Rivers, and by cutting off our subsistence render our arms useless; and to remain here for transports to carry us off would be a work of time, would loose our cavalry, and be otherwise as ruinous and disgraceful

graceful to Britain as moſt events could be. - I have therefore under ſo many embarraſſing circumſtances (but *looking upon Charles-town as ſafe from any immediate attack of the rebels*) reſolved to take advantage of General Greene's having left the back part of Virginia open, and march immediately into that province, to attempt a junction with General Phillips.

I have more readily decided upon this meaſure, becauſe if General Greene fails in the object of his march, his retreat will relieve South Carolina; and my force being very inſufficient for offenſive operations in this province, may be employed uſefully in Virginia, in conjunction with the corps under the command of General Phillips.

I have the honour, &c.

(Signed) CORNWALLIS.

Copy. — From Earl Cornwallis to Sir Henry Clinton, dated Wilmington, April 24, 1781.

SIR,

I HAVE reflected very ſerioufly on the ſubject of my attempt to march into Virginia, and have in conſequence written a letter to Major-general Phillips,

of

of which I have the honour to inclose a copy to your Excellency.

I have likewise directed Lieutenant-colonel Balfour to send transports and provisions to this port, in case I should find the junction with Major-general Phillips impracticable; and that I should have the mortification of seeing that there is no other method of conveying his Majesty's troops to South Carolina, without exposing them to the most evident danger of being lost.

I have the honour, &c.

(Signed) CORNWALLIS.

Copy. — *From Earl Cornwallis to Major-general Phillips, dated April* 24, 1781.

DEAR PHILLIPS,

MY situation here is very distressing, Greene took the advantage of my being obliged to come to this place, and has marched to South Carolina. My expresses to Lord Rawdon on my leaving Cross Creek, warning him of the possibility of such a movement, have all failed; mountaineers and militia have poured into the back part of that province, and I much fear that Lord Rawdon's posts will be so distant from each other, and his troops so scattered, as to put him in danger of being beat in detail; and that the worst of consequences may happen to most of the troops out of Charles-town.

By a direct move towards Camden I cannot get time enough to relieve Lord Rawdon, and should he have fallen, my army would be exposed to the utmost danger, from the great rivers I should have to pass, the exhausted state of the country, the numerous militia, the almost universal spirit of revolt which prevails in South Carolina, and the strength of Greene's army, whose continentals alone are at least as numerous as I am: and I could be of no use on my arrival at Charles-town, there being nothing at present to apprehend for that post. I shall therefore immediately march up the country by Duplin court house, pointing towards Hillsborough, in hopes to withdraw Greene. If that should not succeed, I should be much tempted to try to make a junction with you. *The attempt is exceedingly hazardous, and many unforeseen difficulties may render it totally impracticable*; so that you must not take any steps that may expose your army to the danger of being ruined. I shall march to the lowest ford of the Roanoke, which I am informed is about twenty miles above Taylor's ferry. Send every possible intelligence to me by the cypher I inclose, and make every movement in your power to facilitate our meeting (which must be somewhere near Petersburg) with safety to your own army. *I mention*

mention the lowest ford, because in a hostile country, ferries cannot be depended upon; but if I should decide upon the measure of endeavouring to come to you, I shall try to surprise the boats at some of the ferries from Halifax, upwards, &c.

(Signed) CORNWALLIS.

Copy.— *From Lieutenant-colonel Balfour to Sir Henry Clinton, K. B. dated Charles-town, May* 6, 1781.

SIR,

IN my letters of the 20th and 23d ultimo, I had the honour to inform your Excellency, that our post at Wright's bluff was invested by the enemy, and the apprehensions I was then under of Camden being in the same situation.

I am now to inform you that the former has since been surrendered. The circumstances which led to this cannot be more fully explained, or with more honour to himself than by Lieutenant Mackay's journal of the siege; which together with the articles of capitulation, I therefore inclose for your Excellency's inspection.

By to-morrow I am in hopes Lord Rawdon will be re-inforced by Lieutenant-colonel Watson, with his corps and the sixty-fourth regiment.

But

But notwithstanding Lord Rawdon's brilliant success, I must inform your Excellency, that the general state of the country is most distressing; that the enemies parties are every where; the communication by land with Savannah no longer exists; Colonel Brown is invested at Augusta; and Colonel Cruger in the most critical situation at Ninety Six, nearly confined to his works, and without any present command over that country. Indeed I should betray the duty I owe your Excellency, did I not represent the defection of this province so universal, that I know of no mode short of depopulation, to retain it. This spirit of revolt is in a great measure kept up by the many officers prisoners of war here; and I should therefore think it advisable to remove them, as well as to make the most striking examples of such, as having taken protection, snatch every occasion to rise in arms against us.

I have the honour, &c.

(Signed) W. BALFOUR.

PART VII.

PART VII.

CONTAINING

EXTRACTS

FROM THE

Correspondence from his Lordship's entering Virginia, &c.

Extract. — *From Sir Henry Clinton, K. B. to Lord Cornwallis, dated New York, May 29, 1781.*

MY LORD,

I HAD the honour of writing to your Lordship by Lord Chewton, who sailed from hence in the Richmond the 4th instant to join you at Wilmington. But your Lordship's departure from thence will have prevented his meeting you there, and I hope he has since then joined you in the Chesapeak.

When

When I firſt heard of your Lordſhip's retreat from Croſs Creek to Wilmington, I confeſs that I was in hopes you had reaſon to conſider Greene ſo totally hors de combat as to be perfectly at eaſe for Lord Rawdon's ſafety. And after your arrival at Wilmington, I flattered myſelf that if any change of circumſtances ſhould make it neceſſary, you could always have been able to march to the Walkamaw, where I imagined veſſels might have paſſed you over to George town. I cannot therefore conceal from your Lordſhip the apprehenſions I felt on reading your letter to me of the 24th ultimo; wherein you informed me of the critical ſituation which you ſuppoſed the Carolinas to be in; and that you ſhould probably attempt to effect a junction with Major general Phillips. Lord Rawdon's officer-like and ſpirited exertions, in taking advantage of Greene's having detached from his army, have indeed eaſed me of my apprehenſions for the preſent. But in the diſordered ſtate of Carolina and Georgia, as repreſented to me by Lieutenant-colonel Balfour, I ſhall dread what may be the conſequence of your Lordſhip's move; unleſs a reinforcement arrives very ſoon in South Carolina, and ſuch inſtructions are ſent to the officer commanding there, as may induce him to exert himſelf in reſtoring tranquility to that province at leaſt. Theſe, I make no doubt your Lordſhip has already ſent to Lord Rawdon, and that every neceſſary meaſure for this purpoſe

pose will be taken by his Lordship in confequence of them, fhould he remain in the command. ———

——— Had it been poffible for your Lordfhip, in your letter of the 10th ultimo, to have intimated the probability of your intention to form a junction with General Phillips, I certainly fhould have endeavoured to have ftopped you ——— as I did then, as well as now, confider fuch a move as like to be dangerous to our interefts in the fouthern colonies. And this, my Lord, was not my only fear. For I will be free to own that I was apprehenfive for the corps under your Lordfhip's immediate orders, as well as for that under Lord Rawdon. And I fhould not have thought even the one under Major-general Phillips in fafety at Peterfburg, at leaft for fo long a time, had I not fortunately on hearing of your being at Wilmington, fent another detachment from this army, to reinforce him.

I am perfuaded your Lordfhip will have the goodnefs to excufe my faying thus much. But what is done cannot now be altered. And as your Lordfhip has thought proper to make this decifion, I fhall moft gladly avail myfelf of your very able affiftance, in carrying on fuch operations *as you fhall judge beft in Virginia*, until we are compelled, as I fear we muft be, by the climate, to bring them more northward. Your Lordfhip will have been informed of my ideas refpecting operations to the northward of the Carolinas, by my inftructions to the different General officers

cers detached to the Chefapeak, and the fubftance of fome converfations with General Phillips on the fubject, which I committed to writing, and fent to him with my laft difpatch, with directions to communicate it to your Lordfhip. By thefe your Lordfhip will obferve that my firft object has been to co-operate with your meafures. But your Lordfhip's fituation at different periods made it neceffary for me occafionally to vary my inftructions to thofe General officers, according to circumftances. They were originally directed to affift your Lordfhip's operations in fecuring South and recovering North Carolina; their attention was afterwards pointed to the faving South Carolina.

And now, your Lordfhip may think it neceffary to employ your force in recovering both or either of thefe provinces, by either a direct or indirect operation. With refpect to the firft your Lordfhip muft be fole judge. With refpect to the laft you have my opinions. *My opinions may however probably give way to yours fhould they differ from them, as they will have the advantage of being formed on the fpot, and upon circumftances which at this diftance I cannot of courfe judge of. I fhall therefore leave them totally to your Lordfhip to decide upon, till you either hear from me or we meet.*

I fhould be happy to be able to afcertain the time when our reinforcements may arrive; but as I have received no letters from the minifter of a later date

than

than the 7th of February, I am at a lofs to guefs how foon we may expect them. As I had judged the force I fent to the Chefapeak fully fufficient for all operations there, even though we fhould extend them to the experiment (mentioned in the converfations referred to) at the weftern head of the Chefapeak, about Baltimore, &c. And your Lordfhip will perceive that it was General Phillips and Arnold's opinion they were fufficient for even that on the eaftern, (which however might certainly require a greater force), it is poffible that the additional corps your Lordfhip has brought with you may enable you to return fomething to me for this poft. But I beg your Lordfhip will by no means confider this as a call — for I fhould rather content myfelf with ever fo bare a defenfive, until there was an appearance of ferious operation againft me, than cramp your's in the leaft. But (as I faid in a former letter) I truft to your Lordfhip's difinterestednefs, that you will not require from me more troops than what are abfolutely wanted; and that you will recollect a circumftance, which I am ever aware of, in carrying on operations in the Chefapeak ; *which is that they can be no longer fecure than while we are fuperior at fea.* That we fhall remain fo I moft fincerely *hope* — nor have I any reafon to fufpect we fhall not ; but at all events I may at leaft expect timely information will be fent me of the contrary being likely to happen. In which cafe I hope your Lordfhip may be able *to place your army in a fecure a secure situation during such temporary inconvenience.* For should it become permanent, I need not say what our prospects in this country are likely to be. The admiral being now off the Hook gives me an opportunity of communicating with him by letter, and I have in the most pressing terms requested his attention to the Chesapeak; having repeatedly told him, that should the *enemy possess it even for forty-eight hours, your Lordship's operations there may be exposed to most imminent danger.* General Robertson has also endeavoured to impress him with the same ideas. But until I have an answer in writing, I cannot be sure that he will, as I do, consider the Chesapeak as the first object: For he at present seems rather inclined to lead his fleet to open the port of Rhode-island, and to cruise to the northward of Nantucket for a fleet, which he has heard is coming from Europe with a small reinforcement to the French armament, and which I am of opinion is bound to Rhode-island. I have however taken every occasion to represent to him the necessity of hearty co-operation and communication. If they fail, I am determined it shall not be on my side.

I have the honour, &c.

(Signed) H. CLINTON.

[Sent by Lieutenant-colonel M'Pherson, in the Loyalist, June 15.]

Extract.

Extract. — From Earl Cornwallis to Sir Henry Clinton, K. B. dated Bird's Plantation, North of James-river, May 26, 1781.

SIR,

THE arrival of the reinforcement has made me eafy about Portfmouth for the prefent. I have fent General Leflie thither with the feventeenth regiment, and the two battalions of Anfpach, keeping the forty-third regiment with the army.

I fhall now proceed to diflodge La Fayette from Richmond, and with my light troops to deftroy any magazines or ftores in the neighbourhood, which may have been collected either for his ufe, or for General Greene's army. From thence I purpofe to move to the neck at Williamfburgh, which is reprefented as healthy, and where fome fubfiftence may be procured; and keep myfelf unengaged from operations, which might interfere with your plan for the campaign, until I have the fatisfaction of hearing from you. I hope I fhall then have an opportunity to receive better information than has hitherto been in my power to procure, relative to a proper harbour and place of arms. At prefent I am inclined to think well of York. The objections to Portfmouth are, that it cannot be made ftrong without an army to defend it; that it is remarkably unhealthy; and can

give

give no protection to a ship of the line. Wayne has not yet joined La Fayette, nor can I positively learn where he is, or what is his force. Greene's cavalry are said to be coming this way; but I have no certain accounts of it.

Your Excellency desires Generals Phillips and Arnold to give you their opinions relative to Mr. ———'s proposal. As General Arnold goes to New-York by the first safe conveyance, you will have an opportunity of hearing his sentiments in person. Experience has made me less sanguine, and more arrangements seem to me necessary for so important an expedition than appears to occur to General Arnold.

Mr. ———'s conversations bear too great a resemblance to those of the emissaries from North Carolina, to give me much confidence; and from the experience I have had, and the dangers I have undergone, one maxim appears to me to be absolutely necessary for the safe and honourable conduct of this war; which is, that we should have as few posts as possible; and that wherever the King's troops are, they should be in respectable force. By the vigorous exertions of the present governors of America, large bodies of men are soon collectd, and I have too often observed, that when a storm threatens, our friends disappear.

In regard to taking possession of Philadelphia by an incursion (even if practicable) without an intention
of

of keeping or burning it, (neither of which appear to be adviseable) I should apprehend it would do more harm than good to the cause of Britain.

I shall take the liberty of repeating, that if offensive war is intended, Virginia appears to me to be the only province in which it can be carried on; and in which there is a stake. But to reduce the province and keep possession of the country, a considerable army would be necessary; for with a small force, the business would probably terminate unfavourably, though the beginning might be successful. In case it is thought expedient, and a proper army for the attempt can be formed; I hope your Excellency will do me the justice to believe, that I neither wish nor expect to have the command of it, leaving you at New York on the defensive. Such sentiments are so far from my heart, that I can with great truth assure you, that few things could give me greater pleasure, than being relieved by your presence, from a situation of so much anxiety and responsibility.

By my letter of the 20th, your Excellency will observe, that instead of thinking it possible to do any thing in North Carolina, I am of opinion that it is doubtful whether we can keep the posts in the back parts of South Carolina. And I believe I have stated in former letters, the infinite difficulty of protecting a frontier of three hundred miles, against a persevering enemy, in a country where we have no water communication,

munication, and where few of the inhabitants are active or useful friends.

In enumerating the corps employed in the southern district, your Excellency will recollect that they are all very weak; and that some of the British as well as Provincial regiments, retain nothing but the name. Our weakness at Guildford was not owing to any detachment, unless that with the baggage, but to losses by action, sickness, &c. during the winter's campaign.

Extract.—*Sir Henry Clinton, K. B. to Lord Cornwallis, dated New-York, June* 11, 1781.

RESPECTING my opinions of stations in James and York rivers, I shall beg leave only to refer your Lordship to my instructions to, and correspondence with, Generals Phillips and Arnold, together with the substance of my conversations with the former; which your Lordship will have found amongst General Phillips's papers, and to which I referred you in my last dispatch; I shall therefore of course approve of any alterations your Lordship may think proper to make in those stations.

The detachments I have made from this army into Chesapeak since General Leslie's expedition in October last, inclusive, have amounted to seven thousand seven hundred and twenty-four effectives; and at the time your Lordship made the junction with the corps there, there were under Major-general Phillips's orders, five thousand three hundred and four. A force, I should have hoped would be sufficient of itself to carry on any operations in any of the southern provinces in America.

—— comparing, therefore the force under your Lordship, and that of the enemy opposed to you (and I think it clearly appears they have, for the present, no intention of sending thither reinforcement) I should have hoped you would have quite sufficient to carry on any operation in Virginia — should that have been advisable in this advanced season.

By the intercepted letters inclosed to your Lordship in my last dispatch, you will observe, that I am threatened with a siege in this post. My present effective force is only ten thousand nine hundred and thirty-one. With respect to what the enemy may collect for such an object, it is probable they may amount to at least twenty thousand; besides reinforcement to the French (which from pretty good authority, I have reason to expect) and the numerous militia of the five neighbouring provinces.

Thus

Thus circumstanced, I am persuaded your Lordship will be of opinion, that the sooner I concentrate my force the better. Therefore, (unless your Lordship, after the receipt of my letters of the 29th of May and 8th inst. should incline to agree with me in opinion, and judge it right to adopt my ideas respecting the move to Baltimore, or the Delaware Neck, &c.) I beg leave to recommend it to you, as soon as you have finished the active operations you may be now engaged in, to take a defensive station in any healthy situation you choose (be it at Williamsburgh or York town) and I would wish in that case, that after reserving to yourself such troops as you may judge necessary for an ample defensive, and desultory movements by water, for the purpose of annoying the enemy's communications, destroying magazines, &c. the following corps may be sent to me in succession, as you can spare them:

 Two battalions of light infantry.
 Forty-third regiment.
 Seventy-sixth, or eightieth.
 Two battalions of Anspach.
 Queen's rangers, cavalry and infantry.
 Remains of the detachment of the seventeenth light dragoons.

And such a proportion of artillery as can be spared, particularly men.

Copy. — *Sir Henry Clinton, K. B. to Lord Cornwallis, dated New-York, June* 15, 1781.

MY LORD,

As the Admiral has thought proper to stop the sailing of the convoy with stores, horse, accoutrements, &c. (which has been for some days ready to sail to the Chesapeak) without assigning to me any reason for so doing, I delay not a moment to dispatch a runner to your Lordship with a duplicate of my letter of the 11th inst. which was to go by that opportunity. And as I am led to suppose from your Lordship's letter of the 26th ultimo, that you may not think it expedient to adopt the operations I had recommended in the Chesapeak, and will by this time probably have finished those you were engaged in; I request you will immediately embark a part of the troops, stated in the letter inclosed; beginning with the light infantry; and send them to me with all possible dispatch; for which purpose Captain Hudson, or officer commanding the king's ships, will, I presume, upon your Lordship's application appoint a proper convoy. I shall likewise, in proper time, solicit the admiral to send some more transports to the Chesapeak; in which your Lordship will please to send hither the remaining troops you judge can be spared from the defence of the posts you may occupy, as I do not think it adviseable to leave more troops in that unhealthy climate, at this season of the year, than what are absolutely wanted for a defensive, and desultory water excursions.

H. CLINTON,

Extract. — *Lord Cornwallis to Sir Henry Clinton, K. B. dated Williamsbugrh, June* 30, 1781.

―――― BEING in the place of General Phillips, I thought myself called upon by you, to give my opinion, with all deference, on Mr. ――――'s proposals, and the attempt upon Philadelphia. Having experienced much disappointment on that head, I own I would cautiously engage in measures, depending materially for their success, upon active assistance from the country. And I thought the attempt on Philadelphia would do more harm than good to the cause of Great Britain.

―――― However, my opinion on that subject is at present of no great importance, as it appears from your Excellency's dispatches, that in the execution of those ideas, a co-operation was intended from your side; which now could not be depended upon from the uncertainty of the permancy of our naval superiority, and your apprehensions of an intended serious attempt upon New York.

END OF THE APPENDIX.

Return of intrenching Tools in the poſſeſſion of the Engineers at York Town, in Virginia on the 23d of Auguſt, 1781.

Spades and ſhovels	-	-	-	400
Pick-axes	-	-	-	190
Felling-axes	-	-	-	210
Hand-hatchets	-	-	-	160
Wheel-barrows	-	-	-	32
				992

New-York,   OL. DE LANCY,
Dec. 27, 1781.   ADJUTANT-GENERAL.

N. B. This return formed from different returns, ſigned by Lieutenant Sutherland, Lord Cornwallis's principal Engineer in the Cheſapeak.

CPSIA information can be obtained
at www.ICGtesting.com
Printed in the USA
LVHW021630310323
743145LV00003B/467

9 781342 13404